Introduction to Connections
Grades 3–5

Honi J. Bamberger
Christine Oberdorf

The Math Process Standards Series
Susan O'Connell, Series Editor

HEINEMANN
Portsmouth, NH

D0905784

Heinemann
A division of Reed Elsevier Inc.
361 Hanover Street
Portsmouth, NH 03801–3912
www.heinemann.com

Offices and agents throughout the world

The authors and publisher wish to thank those who have generously given permission to reprint borrowed material:

Excerpts from *Principles and Standards for School Mathematics*. Copyright © 2000 by the National Council of Teachers of Mathematics. Reprinted with permission. All rights reserved.

Library of Congress Cataloging-in-Publication Data
Bamberger, Honi Joyce.
  Introduction to connections : grades 3–5 / Honi J. Bamberger, Christine Oberdorf.
    p. cm.—(The math process standards series)
  Includes bibliographical references.
  ISBN-13: 978-0-325-00999-5
  ISBN-10: 0-325-00999-6
  1. Mathematics—Study and teaching (Elementary)—United States.
2. Mathematics—Study and teaching (Elementary)—Evaluation.
3. Curriculum planning.   I. Oberdorf, Christine.   II. Title.
  QA135.6.B36 2007
  372.7—dc22   2006029096

Editor: Emily Michie Birch
Production: Elizabeth Valway
Cover design: Night & Day Design
Composition: Publishers' Design and Production Services, Inc.
CD production: Nicole Russell and Marla Berry
Manufacturing: Jamie Carter

Printed in the United States of America on acid-free paper
  11 10 09 08 07   ML   1 2 3 4 5

To all of the teachers who have allowed us into their classrooms for the past fifteen years. We have loved working with you and working with your students.

To our families, friends, and colleagues, who constantly inspire and believe in us.

And especially to Aley, Robert, Stephanie, and Jessica, who provide us with reasons for wanting teachers to be the best that they can be.

In order to be effective mathematicians, students need to develop understanding of critical math content. They need to understand number and operations, algebra, measurement, geometry, and data analysis and probability. Through continued study of these content domains, students gain a comprehensive understanding of mathematics as a subject with varied and interconnected concepts. As math teachers, we attempt to provide students with exposure to, exploration in, and reflection about the many skills and concepts that make up the study of mathematics.

Even with a deep understanding of math content, however, students may lack important skills that can assist them in their development as effective mathematicians. Along with content knowledge, students need an understanding of the processes used by mathematicians. They must learn to problem solve, communicate their ideas, reason through math situations, prove their conjectures, make connections between and among math concepts, and represent their mathematical thinking. Development of content alone does not provide students with the means to explore, express, or apply that content. As we strive to develop effective mathematicians, we are challenged to develop both students' content understanding and process skills.

The National Council of Teachers of Mathematics (2000) has outlined critical content and process standards in its *Principles and Standards for School Mathematics* document. These standards have become the road map for the development of textbooks, curriculum materials, and student assessments. These standards have provided a framework for thinking about what needs to be taught in math classrooms and how various skills and concepts can be blended together to create a seamless math curriculum. The first five standards outline content standards and expectations related to number and operations, algebra, geometry, measurement, and data analysis and probability. The second five standards outline the process goals of problem solving, reasoning and proof, communication, connections, and representations. A strong understanding of these standards empowers teachers to identify and select activities within their curricula to produce powerful learning. The standards provide a vision for what teachers hope their students will achieve.

This book is a part of a vital series designed to assist teachers in understanding the NCTM Process Standards and the ways in which they impact and guide student learning. An additional goal of this series is to provide practical ideas to support teachers as they ensure that the acquisition of process skills has a critical place in their math instruction. Through this series, teachers will gain an understanding of each process standard as well as gather ideas for bringing that standard to life within their math classrooms. It offers practical ideas for lesson development, implementation, and assessment that work with any curriculum. Each book in the series focuses on a critical process skill in a highlighted grade band and all books are designed to encourage reflection about teaching and learning. The series also highlights the interconnected nature of the process and content standards by showing correlations between them and showcasing activities that address multiple standards.

Students who develop an understanding of content skills and cultivate the process skills that allow them to apply that content understanding become effective mathematicians. Our goal as teachers is to support and guide students as they develop both their content knowledge and their process skills, so they are able to continue to expand and refine their understanding of mathematics. This series is a guide for math educators who aspire to teach students more than math content. It is a guide to assist teachers in understanding and teaching the critical processes through which students learn and make sense of mathematics.

Susan O'Connell
Series Editor

Many people have contributed in important ways to the development of this book and some of the work upon which it is based. We would like to thank Ms. Lyons, Ms. Williams, and Ms. Brooks, teachers at Govans Elementary School, in Baltimore City, Maryland, who allowed us into their classrooms to work with and photograph their students. The same gratitude is extended to Ms. Lozzi, Ms. Brown, Ms. Anderson, and Ms. Gibney, teachers at Oak View Elementary School, in Silver Spring, Maryland. Ms. Melanie Peck, teacher at The Summit School, in Edgewater, Maryland, not only allowed us into her classroom, but provided us with the complete story of Elizabeth's garden. We would like to thank Ms. Tammy Fant, math coach from Decatur City Schools, who shared with us work that she did with third graders. We would like to thank Mr. Keith Gallagher, who created and shared some of the CD activities with us. Susan O'Connell inspired and guided us as we worked on this project. Thanks also go to our editor, Emily Birch, who constantly provided us with positive feedback and kept us motivated.

Problem-Solving Standard

Instructional programs from prekindergarten through grade 12 should enable all students to—

■ build new mathematical knowledge through problem solving;

■ solve problems that arise in mathematics and in other contexts;

■ apply and adapt a variety of appropriate strategies to solve problems;

■ monitor and reflect on the process of mathematical problem solving.

Reasoning and Proof Standard

Instructional programs from prekindergarten through grade 12 should enable all students to—

■ recognize reasoning and proof as fundamental aspects of mathematics;

■ make and investigate mathematical conjectures;

■ develop and evaluate mathematical arguments and proofs;

■ select and use various types of reasoning and methods of proof.

---

* Standards are listed with the permission of the National Council of Teachers of Mathematics (NCTM). NCTM does not endorse the content or validity of these alignments.

Communication Standard

Instructional programs from prekindergarten through grade 12 should enable all students to—

- organize and consolidate their mathematical thinking through communication;

- communicate their mathematical thinking coherently and clearly to peers, teachers, and others;

- analyze and evaluate the mathematical thinking and strategies of others;

- use the language of mathematics to express mathematical ideas precisely.

Connections Standards

Instructional programs from prekindergarten through grade 12 should enable all students to—

- recognize and use connections among mathematical ideas;

- understand how mathematical ideas interconnect and build on one another to produce a coherent whole;

- recognize and apply mathematics in contexts outside of mathematics.

Representation Standard

Instructional programs from prekindergarten through grade 12 should enable all students to—

- create and use representations to organize, record, and communicate mathematical ideas;

- select, apply, and translate among mathematical representations to solve problems;

- use representations to model and interpret physical, social, and mathematical phenomena.

NCTM Content Standards and Expectations for Grades 3–5

NUMBER AND OPERATIONS

	Expectations
Instructional programs from prekindergarten through grade 12 should enable all students to—	**In grades 3–5 all students should—**
understand numbers, ways of representing numbers, relationships among numbers, and number systems	• understand the place-value structure of the base-ten number system and be able to represent and compare whole numbers and decimals; • recognize equivalent representations for the same number and generate them by decomposing and composing numbers; • develop understanding of fractions as parts of unit wholes, as parts of a collection, as locations on number lines, and as divisions of whole numbers; • use models, benchmarks, and equivalent forms to judge the size of fractions; • recognize and generate equivalent forms of commonly used fractions, decimals, and percents; • explore numbers less than 0 by extending the number line and through familiar applications; • describe classes of numbers according to characteristics such as the nature of their factors.
understand meanings of operations and how they relate to one another	• understand various meanings of multiplication and division; • understand the effects of multiplying and dividing whole numbers; • identify and use relationships between operations, such as division as the inverse of multiplication, to solve problems; • understand and use properties of operations, such as the distributivity of multiplication over addition.

| | Expectations |
Instructional programs from prekindergarten through grade 12 should enable all students to—	In grades 3–5 all students should—
compute fluently and make reasonable estimates	• develop fluency with basic number combinations for multiplication and division and use these combinations to mentally compute related problems, such as 30×50; • develop fluency in adding, subtracting, multiplying, and dividing whole numbers; • develop and use strategies to estimate the results of whole-number computations and to judge the reasonableness of such results; • develop and use strategies to estimate computations involving fractions and decimals in situations relevant to students' experience; • use visual models, benchmarks, and equivalent forms to add and subtract commonly used fractions and decimals; • select appropriate methods and tools for computing with whole numbers from among mental computation, estimation, calculators, and paper and pencil according to the context and nature of the computation and use the selected method or tools.

ALGEBRA

| | Expectations |
Instructional programs from prekindergarten through grade 12 should enable all students to—	In grades 3–5 all students should—
understand patterns, relations, and functions	• describe, extend, and make generalizations about geometric and numeric patterns; • represent and analyze patterns and functions, using words, tables, and graphs.

	Expectations
Instructional programs from prekindergarten through grade 12 should enable all students to—	**In grades 3–5 all students should—**
represent and analyze mathematical situations and structures using algebraic symbols	• identify such properties as commutativity, associativity, and distributivity and use them to compute with whole numbers; • represent the idea of a variable as an unknown quantity using a letter or a symbol; • express mathematical relationships using equations.
use mathematical models to represent and understand quantitative relationships	• model problem situations with objects and use representations such as graphs, tables, and equations to draw conclusions.
analyze change in various contexts	• investigate how a change in one variable relates to a change in a second variable; • identify and describe situations with constant or varying rates of change and compare them.

GEOMETRY

	Expectations
Instructional programs from prekindergarten through grade 12 should enable all students to—	**In grades 3–5 all students should—**
analyze characteristics and properties of two- and three-dimensional geometric shapes and develop mathematical arguments about geometric relationships	• identify, compare, and analyze attributes of two- and three-dimensional shapes and develop vocabulary to describe the attributes; • classify two- and three-dimensional shapes according to their properties and develop definitions of classes of shapes such as triangles and pyramids; • investigate, describe, and reason about the results of subdividing, combining, and transforming shapes; • explore congruence and similarity;

	Expectations
Instructional programs from prekindergarten through grade 12 should enable all students to—	**In grades 3–5 all students should—**
	• make and test conjectures about geometric properties and relationships and develop logical arguments to justify conclusions
specify locations and describe spatial relationships using coordinate geometry and other representational systems	• describe location and movement using common language and geometric vocabulary;
	• make and use coordinate systems to specify locations and to describe paths;
	• find the distance between points along horizontal and vertical lines of a coordinate system.
apply transformations and use symmetry to analyze mathematical situations	• predict and describe the results of sliding, flipping, and turning two-dimensional shapes;
	• describe a motion or a series of motions that will show that two shapes are congruent;
	• identify and describe line and rotational symmetry in two- and three-dimensional shapes and designs.
use visualization, spatial reasoning, and geometric modeling to solve problems	• build and draw geometric objects;
	• create and describe mental images of objects, patterns, and paths;
	• identify and build a three-dimensional object from two-dimensional representations of that object;
	• identify and draw a two-dimensional representation of a three-dimensional object;
	• use geometric models to solve problems in other areas of mathematics, such as number and measurement;
	• recognize geometric ideas and relationships and apply them to other disciplines and to problems that arise in the classroom or in everyday life.

	Expectations
Instructional programs from prekindergarten through grade 12 should enable all students to—	**In grades 3–5 all students should—**
understand measurable attributes of objects and the units, systems, and processes of measurement	• understand such attributes as length, area, weight, volume, and size of angle and select the appropriate type of unit for measuring each attribute; • understand the need for measuring with standard units and become familiar with standard units in the customary and metric systems; • carry out simple unit conversions, such as from centimeters to meters, within a system of measurement; • understand that measurements are approximations and how differences in units affect precision; • explore what happens to measurements of a two-dimensional shape such as its perimeter and area when the shape is changed in some way.
apply appropriate techniques, tools, and formulas to determine measurements	• develop strategies for estimating the perimeters, areas, and volumes of irregular shapes; • select and apply appropriate standard units and tools to measure length, area, volume, weight, time, temperature, and the size of angles; • select and use benchmarks to estimate measurements; • develop, understand, and use formulas to find the area of rectangles and related triangles and parallelograms; • develop strategies to determine the surface areas and volumes of rectangular solids.

DATA ANALYSIS AND PROBABILITY

	Expectations
Instructional programs from prekindergarten through grade 12 should enable all students to—	**In grades 3–5 all students should—**
formulate questions that can be addressed with data and collect, organize, and display relevant data to answer them	• design investigations to address a question and consider how data-collection methods affect the nature of the data set; • collect data using observations, surveys, and experiments;
select and use appropriate statistical methods to analyze data	• represent data using tables and graphs such as line plots, bar graphs, and line graphs; • recognize the differences in representing categorical and numerical data. • describe the shape and important features of a set of data and compare related data sets, with an emphasis on how the data are distributed; • use measures of center, focusing on the median, and understand what each does and does not indicate about the data set; • compare different representations of the same data and evaluate how well each representation shows important aspects of the data.
develop and evaluate inferences and predictions that are based on data	• propose and justify conclusions and predictions that are based on data and design studies to further investigate the conclusions or predictions.
understand and apply basic concepts of probability	• describe events as likely or unlikely and discuss the degree of likelihood using such words as *certain, equally likely,* and *impossible;* • predict the probability of outcomes of simple experiments and test the predictions; • understand that the measure of the likelihood of an event can be represented by a number from 0 to 1.

The Connections Standard

Through instruction that emphasizes the interrelatedness of mathematical ideas, students not only learn mathematics, they also learn about the utility of mathematics.

—National Council of Teachers of Mathematics,
Principles and Standards for School Mathematics

Why Focus on Connections?

Many students view mathematics as a collection of isolated skills and concepts that they must work on, in school, to satisfy the requirements for their current grade level. Often textbooks, which provide teachers with a guide for instruction, include a week of study on some skill, only to move on, in the next chapter, to some new skill unrelated to what was just introduced. A week of study on multiplication may be followed by several days of exploring the area of rectangles, just before proceeding to ideas about fractions. This may cause some students to see mathematics as a fragmented, linear progression of skills like an unassembled puzzle. A goal of mathematics education "is to present mathematics as a unified discipline, a woven fabric rather than a patchwork of discrete topics" (NCTM 1995, vii). Imagine how empowered students would be if they could begin linking the pieces of the puzzle together to reveal a more focused picture of mathematics.

In this picture, knowledge of the array model of multiplication could be connected to determining the area of a polygon. It could also provides a visual representation for explaining the multiplication algorithm. And, the multiplication table could be investigated in a manner that provides insights into equivalent fractions. The National Council of Teachers of Mathematics states, "These connections help students see mathematics as a unified body of knowledge rather than a set of complex and disjoint concepts, procedures, and processes" (NCTM 2000, 200).

This is not to say that students are considered unsuccessful in mathematics if they fail to recognize connections. What it does mean is that success is often isolated to specific skills or situations and, in many cases, is short-lived. Our role as educators, therefore, is to be mindful of the multifaceted nature of mathematics and to bring such connections to light, in the classroom.

There are numerous benefits for students who recognize connections among mathematical ideas, between mathematics and other disciplines, and in life experiences. When students understand the interrelatedness of mathematics they often have many more strategies available to them when solving problems, and insights into mathematical relationships (Cobb et al. 1991). These students often develop their own procedures, based on an understanding of place value ideas, rather than mimic a particular strategy or algorithm to reach a solution. Additionally, when students construct knowledge and form connections, they are more likely to transfer conceptual knowledge and apply it to new situations. A deeper level of understanding equates to greater utility and versatility of the knowledge by the learner. The more connections students are able to recognize, the deeper the level of sense making. It is "when students can connect mathematical ideas, [that] their understanding is deeper and more lasting" (NCTM 2000, 64). These connections attribute to a strong and cohesive foundation of knowledge, a fundamental necessity on which to build future knowledge and lifelong understanding.

Children often create connections, on their own, based on their real-life experiences. A Family Circus cartoon (Keane 1994) shows a young boy looking at an analog clock that has the hour hand near the three and the minute hand on the ten. The child says, "The big hand is on channel 10, and the little hand is on channel 3." While sweet and somewhat funny, the implication is that children look for ways to connect what they know with new things that they are learning.

At the conclusion of a lesson, in a third-grade classroom, on a Friday afternoon, the following question was posed, "How might you use mathematics over the weekend?" After a considerable amount of prodding and waiting these responses were given:

> "I'll use math when I do my math homework."
> "I might watch my sister do her math homework."
> "My mom might ask me a basic fact, like 3 times 7."
> "I could count the steps to my room."

That was it! This revealed that these students neither recognized the utility of the mathematics lessons just completed, nor the application of mathematics to their own lives. It seemed that they just believed that mathematics was a subject they learned in school. And that unless mathematics was connected to school (through homework or some other means of practice), they wouldn't be doing mathematics over their weekend. As teachers we need to work hard to provide opportunities for students to recognize and celebrate the connections within mathematics and to their lives—now, and in the future. Many of these efforts are shared, with you, in this book.

What Is the Connection Process Standard?

The National Council of Teachers of Mathematics (NCTM) has developed standards to support and guide teachers' planning for mathematics instruction. These standards include guidelines for instruction in both content and process. The content standards define specific topics of mathematics, while the process standards identify the modes by which students engage in mathematics. The process standards include problem solving, reasoning and proof, communication, connections, and representation. The components of the NCTM Connections Process Standard, the focus of this book, are described by the following expectations (NCTM 2000, 64):

Instructional programs should enable students to—

- recognize and use connections among mathematical ideas

- understand how mathematical ideas interconnect and build on one another to produce a coherent whole

- recognize and apply mathematics in contexts outside of mathematics.

This book explores strategies, activities, and materials designed to assist students in developing a more comprehensive understanding of mathematics by focusing on the connected nature of the subject. Each of the three focuses within connections are covered, and a multitude of resources for classroom use are offered.

The first focus is on the connections that exist among the various content areas that teachers introduce and reinforce during mathematics instruction. Seldom, even in a textbook lesson, are skills taught in isolation from other mathematics topics being learned or reviewed. This is especially true when "rich tasks" and interesting problem-based situations are given to students. One need only look at a "typical" logic problem to see how easy it can be to connect mathematics ideas. (See What Number Am I? in the Mathematical Ideas Interconnect and Build Upon One Another section of the CD.)

What Number Am I?

> I have exactly five digits.
> Each digit is different.
> I am even.
> I am a multiple of ten.
> The sum of the digits in the ones and thousands place is 8.
> The digit in the tens place is $\frac{1}{2}$ of the digit in the thousands place.
> The digit in the ten thousands place is the first prime number.
> The digit in the hundreds place is three squared.
> What Number Am I? ____ ____, ____ ____ ____

Did you follow the clues to solve the puzzle? Did you get 28,940? And, did you see all of the mathematics that a student would get practice with in solving a problem like this one?

There are so many important vocabulary words that get reinforced in the context of this problem (*digit, sum, multiple, prime number, square number, even,* and *exactly*). Knowing the meaning of these terms is important, but equally important is knowing what to do with these words. If the term *sum* is given, students must know that they will be adding. And, they need a strategy for getting this sum. Just knowing the term *multiple* doesn't help a student, unless they understand how to find multiples of ten. This particular logic problem also requires a fairly thorough understanding of place value. All of these skills fall within NCTM's Number and Operation content standard (NCTM 2000). When a teacher makes connections among mathematics concepts and skills, many ideas can be reinforced at the same time.

The second focus is on the connections that exist within the numerous skills and concepts within mathematics itself, and how mathematical ideas interconnect and build on one another. One example of such a connection would be helping students recognize that $\frac{1}{2}$ can be written as the decimal 0.5, and this decimal fraction could define the likelihood of tossing an odd number on a 1–6 numeral cube. These types of connections require an understanding that mathematical ideas interconnect and build upon one another to produce a coherent whole field of study.

In geometry, for example, early studies of triangles and rectangles allow students to derive a formula for the area of a triangle in later grades. And, knowing this allows learners to understand how to find the volume of a triangular prism. For these things to happen, teachers must understand how essential these prerequisite understandings are for later mathematical understandings. But, it is also critical for students to make these connections in order to fully comprehend how earlier understandings make sense when new concepts are presented.

A third focus is to explore the connection between mathematics and other areas of the elementary curriculum. In his chapter on connecting literature and mathematics, David Whitin writes, "an effective strategy for restoring context to mathematical ideas is through the use of children's literature" (NCTM 1995, 134). Not only can mathematical ideas be developed through literature but students' writing can solidify their thinking about strategies used to solve problems. Interdisciplinary approaches to teaching, such as using the mathematics–literature connection, save precious time and also add to students' insight into all curriculum areas involved thereby reinforcing that "The whole is greater than the sum of the parts" (Welchman-Tischler 1992, 1). Spatial awareness and spatial concepts can be integrated into physical education programs; patterns, shapes, and tessellations can be studied in art; and patterns and fractions can be applied in the study of music. Even science and social studies offer a multitude of opportunities to make connections to a variety of mathematics ideas.

While still a part of the connections to other areas of study, a final connection will be made between mathematics and the real world. When money is studied without relating it to getting an allowance, going shopping, and saving to purchase something special, sense-making opportunities are lost. Students need to wonder why "a manhole cover is circular rather than another shape" or whether working for seven days at $20.00 per day is better than being paid $2.00 for the first day and then having your salary doubled every day for a week (NCTM 2000). These are questions that students need to explore in order to appreciate the applicability of mathematics to their world. Such an understanding can serve as a motivating factor for many young learners, as it provides a rationale for engaging in mathematical explorations.

Developing Skills and Attitudes

Recognizing connections in mathematics requires that students consider this content in a new way. Not only must they grasp the necessity of the skill within a particular lesson but they must also reflect on how this knowledge might relate to past understandings and future experiences. Students are required to think beyond one lesson, one concept, and one application in mathematics. Seeking connections must become a habit of the mind for students. But this process is not instinctive for many students, rather, it is learned. As their teachers, it is our responsibility to model these behaviors for students and provide prompts that promote such behaviors. Questioning is one method of promoting this process. We may pose such questions as:

> How does this relate to yesterday's lesson?
> Would the strategy you developed work with this problem?
> When might this be applicable outside of math class?
> Who might need to know this information?

Our goal in posing such questions is to model for students the types of questions they should be asking of one another and of themselves. Students then become involved in the process of building knowledge and making connections, and thus become more accountable for their learning.

It then becomes our job to facilitate a learning environment in which students feel comfortable engaging in discourse to reveal such connections. We want students to rely on themselves and one another to unveil the interrelationships that exist in and between mathematics throughout the curriculum, and in their real world. This occurs in a classroom where students are engaged and invested in the lesson.

CLASSROOM-TESTED TIP

Think-Pair-Share, a cooperative learning strategy, provides students with time to reflect on a question or problem being asked, without dealing with hands being raised and answers being blurted out. We ask students to silently think (for about ten to fifteen seconds) when a question is asked. Then we have them pair up with the person next to them or across from them to quietly share their thoughts. This allows many students to talk at the same time, and gives those who may not have had an idea about an answer an opportunity to hear what their partner thinks. Then, after about a minute of pairing, students are asked to share (out loud) the things that they've heard or the things they had been thinking about. Students are more invested in the lesson and they are more willing to participate when this strategy is employed.

Additionally, we must choose tasks that are meaningful and accentuate the connections among content areas and extend to other disciplines. This often means that a few activities are explored in depth. Lastly, we must be knowledgeable about students' prior knowledge and know the content and skills to be taught in later grades. We cannot limit our expertise to the particular grade level we teach. Only then may we empower learners to develop a strong, well-connected knowledge base. "Building on connections can make mathematics a challenging, engaging, and exciting domain of study" (NCTM 2000, 205).

The question "How will you use mathematics over the weekend?" will still be one that is asked of students. And, they may still respond with, "I'll be doing my math homework over the weekend." But, we also expect that there will be many other statements that students will make, that let us know that they understand the value of the mathematics they are learning. They might say,

> "I'll be keeping score during our bowling tournament."
> "I'll try to estimate how much our groceries cost at the store this Saturday."
> "As soon as I get up on Saturday I'll be looking at the clock to see what time it is."
> "All you have to do is look around to see that math is everywhere. It's the shapes in buildings, the numbers on speed signs, and in so many things that I do!"

How This Book Will Help You

This book is designed to help you better understand the NCTM process standard of connections. It explores ways to help students make sense out of the connections between mathematics ideas, how these ideas build on one another, and how mathematics can be applied in contexts outside of the mathematics classroom. This book focuses specifically on the mathematical expectations of students in grades 3 through 5, and provides practical ideas for helping students recognize, seek, and apply connections. It offers ideas for creating a classroom environment that acknowledges the numerous connections inherent in the field of mathematics, as well as among mathematics and other areas of the curriculum.

Specific grade levels are not necessarily indicated for each activity. Activities are provided to introduce and reinforce important teacher strategies necessary in creating a learning environment that encourages and applauds the recognition of connections.

Classroom activities are provided to explore the relationship of the content standards and the connections process standard. Examples of student work are included to more clearly illustrate student's understandings based on their ability to make connections. Often these student work samples illustrate their attempt at making sense of the mathematics they've learned in the past and the mathematics being introduced to them presently. Their justification is often a means to explain a particular strategy's effectiveness in reaching a solution, which in turn, opens the door to a variety of connections within mathematics.

The final chapter explores techniques in measuring students' abilities to make connections. Assessment samples take the form of classroom discourse, written formative assessments, and individual conferencing with students. Student responses are provided, as well as conclusions summarizing student knowledge and potential gaps revealed through work samples. Additionally, recommendations for instruction based on the examination of student work serve as suggestions for future instruction.

The accompanying CD includes a variety of teacher-ready materials to aid in the recognition of connections within the mathematics classroom. These resources include specific activities and tasks that highlight the connections within mathematics and the utility of mathematics. Scoring tools, observation sheets, and concept maps are also provided to enhance instruction. The activities span various levels of complexity. Choose tasks based on your students' level of expertise and alignment with your local curriculum. Also, these activities can be adjusted and edited so that you can use your students' names and specific interests.

Lastly, each chapter concludes with questions for discussion. These prompt you to reflect on the content of the chapter, either individually or with a group of colleagues. They offer you an opportunity to engage in discussions about the appropriateness of what has been read and the impact this might have on student understanding. Practical resources are listed to facilitate the implementation of ideas explored throughout the chapters.

The consistent practice of making and applying connections in mathematics contributes to students having a deeper level of mathematical understanding. As educators, we must create an environment in which students are taught to seek out such connections, and thus think like mathematicians, celebrating the relevance and applicability of mathematics.

Questions for Discussion

1. How were connections highlighted and emphasized in the mathematics instruction that you received as a young learner?

2. What learning experiences did you have that helped you make a connection among mathematical ideas, or that strengthened your understanding of a particular concept?

3. If students show competence with computational skills but fail to recognize the connectedness and utility of mathematics, how might this effect their achievement?

4. What changes might you make in your planning or instructional practices to facilitate student recognition of connections? What would you need to do to make these changes a reality?

CHAPTER 1

Connections Among the Content Standards

Through instruction that emphasizes the interrelatedness of mathematical ideas, students not only learn mathematics, they also learn about the utility of mathematics.

—National Council of Teachers of Mathematics,
Principles and Standards for School Mathematics

Foundation Skills and Varied Components of This Standard

What Teachers Need to Understand and Explore to Effectively Address This Standard

We've heard the same lament from teachers all across the country, "How will I ever get through all of the content I'm supposed to teach during the year? There just isn't enough time!"

And, it's true, there isn't; especially in many districts where the amount of time devoted to the teaching of mathematics is less than an hour a day. In fact, many teachers would be thrilled if they *had* an hour a day to teach math. We hear from teachers in many different places across the country that they often have to teach math at the end of the day (when their students are tired), after recess (when their students are tired), or somewhere after their literacy block (when their students are tired). Does this resonate true for you, too?

There really isn't enough time, no matter whether you teach third, fourth, or fifth grade, to do a really good job helping students understand—not merely hear about—

all of the concepts and skills that they are expected to learn. And, the problem becomes even more complex when you realize that children enter third through fifth grade with varying skill levels. You may have a student who is barely able to add multidigit numbers with regrouping, yet you're expected to introduce adding fractions with unlike denominators. And, isn't there often one student who comes in with such a clear understanding of mathematics that you wonder how you'll challenge him or her throughout the year?

Are you smiling and nodding to yourself? Does this sound exactly like your classroom?

There isn't an easy "fix" for this dilemma, especially when you consider that many states are now testing students in February or March, creating the frenzy of teaching everything by the time students get tested. But there is hope! We've found that if teachers carefully select the tasks that they give to students (to introduce and reinforce the concepts and skills at their grade level), making a note of what other mathematics skills and concepts are being reinforced at the same time, that more content is taught—and in a more meaningful manner. And, when there are context problems (Fosnot and Dolk 2001), which are closely connected to children's lives, then genuine understanding will occur.

In addition, when teachers begin to help students look for their own connections among mathematical ideas (i.e., seeing division as repeated subtraction and multiplication as repeated addition) students begin asking themselves, "How is what we're learning right now similar to things we've studied before?"

Consider the following activity (see also Even Odd Product Game in the Connections Among the Content Standards section on the CD). Fourth-grade students are studying probability and are given the following problem:

> **You have two fair numeral cubes (with the digits 1–6). You're playing a game with a friend. Player One gets *a point* when the product tossed is *even*. Player Two gets *a point* when the product tossed is *odd*.**

> **Would you rather be Player One or Player Two?**

After reading the problem, students count off by ones and twos until every student has called out a number. Then they are directed to design an experiment to determine the likelihood of tossing an even versus an odd product as well as use some vehicle to represent their findings. Finally, in a paragraph, they are to explain why they chose the player they would prefer to be.

Before beginning this experiment you need to stimulate a conversation about the mathematics that students need to know in order to do this activity. What are all the mathematical concepts students will be practicing while engaging in this activity?

By asking questions, you're then able to determine whether students have the prerequisite understandings to tackle this task and gain an understanding of what it means for a game to be fair. So, what sorts of questions will give you this information? It's often good to begin with open-ended questions like the following and then use more specific ones as information is given to you from your students.

■ After reading the information about today's experiment, what are some things that you think you need to know to do this successfully? (Students may say that they need to know what *even* means and what *odd* means, as well as the word *product*.)

■ What does it mean for a number to be even? What does it mean for a number to be odd? And, when you are finding the product, what will you be doing?

■ What strategies will you use if you cannot remember a certain multiplication fact?

■ How will you work together to share the work of this experiment?

As important as the mathematics is in this activity you also need to talk with students about what it means to cooperate during a task such as this. We like these questions:

■ What does cooperation look like?

■ What does cooperation sound like?

In classrooms where real collaboration takes place, we hear students saying the most wonderful things about how they will be working together. In response to What does cooperation look like?, we've heard things like:

"Children helping each other."
"Children sharing materials with each other."
"Children taking turns."

In response to What does cooperation sound like?, third graders said:

"May I help you find the materials you need to do this?"
"Thank you for sharing your materials with me."
"I really like the way you solved that problem."

Setting up the environment so that students will be successful ensures a higher level of involvement and often a higher level of understanding.

Before we look at what students did with this activity let's look at all of the mathematics that students will get practice with by doing this experiment. They'll need to have some knowledge of:

■ the difference between an even and an odd number

■ what a product is and what operation is used to get products

■ basic multiplication facts, at least 1×1 to 6×6

■ some strategy for keeping track of their products as they conduct the experiment

■ some mechanism for reporting their findings (whether it be by using a fraction or decimal or by displaying their data in a chart)

■ vocabulary associated with probability (e.g., *likelihood, probable, impossible, often, never, usually*)

There are also some obvious skills they must have; for example, students need to know how to count and compare quantities.

From this Player One/Player Two activity, the teacher can reinforce number and operation concepts and data analysis and probability skills. Writing, to justify one's actions, is incorporated into the activity and various representations will surely be demonstrated. All of this is done through one motivating problem-solving task that fourth-grade students will want to address because they will play this game, and they will want to "win."

To truly connect mathematics from one content standard to another, to look at the big ideas and not isolated skills, we need to take the time to think about all of the mathematics within a task. We need to *really* know the curriculum, both at our own grade level and at the grade level previous to and after ours. In this way we can re-visit skills that some students struggle with, in the context of an engaging activity, or we can move forward, confident that the students understand the skills.

In the previous activity the teacher can revisit the notion of *even* and *odd*, a number concept that is often taught in first and second grade. Basic multiplication facts are usually introduced in the third grade, but students may enter fourth grade without being able to recall those facts. It is likely that students have done other experiments with numeral cubes, in earlier grades, but it is less likely that they have been asked to develop their own way of keeping track.

CLASSROOM-TESTED TIP

A great way to use number generators (cubes) without having them fall on the floor or make a lot of noise when the students are using them is to place the cubes inside a small transparent container with a lid. The cup is shaken and then the container is turned upside down so the numerals are revealed. The number generators never leave the inside of the cup. If noise is a factor, the number generators can be made of foam. Then, not only do you have these secure inside a container, but when they are shaken you don't hear them.

Some of the new concepts and skills that will be introduced through this activity may include:

■ representing the likelihood of an event occurring using fractions

■ looking at all outcomes when two even factors are tossed, two odd factors are tossed, and one even and one odd factor is tossed

■ "proving" why it's better to be Player One (if you want to win at this game)

In the past we would have just done this activity because it was a fun way to introduce the idea of fairness in a probability task. Now, however, we carefully think about all of the mathematics concepts and skills that we can include in our lessons. If we are able to integrate and teach all of the concepts and skills that we are expected to introduce in a year's time, the students will benefit even more.

Let's look at what happened during this lesson: The teacher begins by holding up two large numeral cubes (with the digits 1–6 on each of them). Students are asked what they notice about the cubes and they respond:

"They are yellow and black."

"They're dice."

"They are the same."

"They have three even numbers and three odd numbers on them." (Their response when asked which ones were even and which ones were odd and how they knew which was which.)

Then the students were asked what *fair* means. Students were given 10 seconds to think about their answers, and then were paired up with the person next to them. The students said that *fair* meant that you and someone else got the same thing or the same amount or that no one would get more than the other.

The students then counted off by ones and twos. All of the students who were ones were asked to raise their hand and then all of the number twos do the same thing. The teacher said, "We're going to play a game and the directions will be on the overhead projector." One of the students read the directions out loud and the entire class was asked whether they felt that the game would be a fair game (based on what they said *fair* meant).

Anthony said, "I think that it will be a fair game because there are three even numbers on each number cube and three odd numbers on each number cube. Both cubes have the same thing, so the game will be fair." Veronica raised her hand and said, "Maybe so, but if you look at the multiplication chart that Ms. Brooks has on the wall, there are a whole lot more even numbers than odd numbers." I asked the class whether they understood what Veronica was saying and they did, but several students agreed with Anthony that the game would be fair since there were the same number of even and odd digits on the cubes.

Students were then given the worksheet (Even Odd Product Game recording sheet from the Connections Among the Content Standards section on the CD) and told that they needed to come up with a way to test their hypothesis about whether this game would be fair to both players. All students were engaged. Students got right to work and began shaking the cups with their cubes inside. Some recorded the entire multiplication equation, while others wrote only the product. Still some students wrote the word *Even* or *Odd* and put a tally mark beneath once they saw the digits that appeared (see Figure 1–1).

The students worked for about fifteen minutes (see Figure 1–2) and then the cups were taken away and students shared what happened during this experiment.

Interestingly, everyone agreed that there were more even products than odd products (regardless of whether they were able to have ten turns or thirty). So, when I asked whether they felt that this was a fair game I was very surprised to hear what most said.

Lanell said, and then subsequently wrote, "This game is fair because me and James counted to 5 then dropped the cup. Others didn't do that. So I steel think it is fair because James won." (See Figure 1–4.) What Lanell and James were thinking was that a game was fair if the players played "fairly." It had nothing to do with whether one player had an advantage over another by having the rules be what they were.

Anthony said the same thing. He wrote, "I think this game is fair because there alway a even chanse to get even or odd numbers. There is 3 odd numbers on the dice, and 3 even." (See Figure 1–5.) (So even with playing the game and seeing that there were many more even products than odd products, he still felt that his original idea was true.) Still, he wrote, "To win at this game you need to be even. When you are odd there is less odds and more evens on the multiplication chart. Even will win!!"

EVEN ODD PRODUCT GAME

Design an experiment to figure out whether there's a better chance for Player One (EVEN) to win, or Player Two (ODD) to win.

Keep track of your data so you can prove whether one player has a better chance of winning, every time.

We decided to write on a blank piece of papper and roll the dice

_____

_____

to see whether one player had a better chance of winning than the other player.

Player 1	Player 2	
$9 \times 2 = 18$	$9 \times 3 = 27$	$5 \times 5 = 25$
$9 \times 3 = 12$	$3 \times 5 = 15$	$9 \times 5 = 45$
$4 \times 1 = 4$	$5 \times 1 = 5$	$3 \times 1 = 3$
$3 \times 6 = 18$	$1 \times 1 = 1$	
$2 \times 2 = 4$	$1 \times 9 = 9$	
$4 \times 1 = 4$	$3 \times 3 = 9$	
$6 \times 4 = 24$	$5 \times 3 = 15$	
$5 \times 2 = 10$	$1 \times 5 = 5$	

Figure 1–1 *Student's record of even and odd products*

(continues)

EVEN ODD PRODUCT GAME

Design an experiment to figure out whether there's a better chance for Player One (EVEN) to win, or Player Two (ODD) to win.

Keep track of your data so you can prove whether one player has a better chance of winning, every time.

We decided to ~~just write the product instad of writing the whole multilycation problem. So it won't take up so much space.~~

to see whether one player had a better chance of winning than the other player.

```
24, 12, 30, 12, 6, 6        Even
6, 9, 2, 25, 30, 3, 20      LHT  HHT    LHT  HHT HHT
13, 2, 8, 6, 13, 15, 15, 6
30, 30, 4, 4, 10, 5, 8
, 6, 16, 4, 4               25 points
```

Figure 1–1 *Continued*

But, Lanell's partner, James, seems convinced that being Player One has a distinct advantage over being Player Two. "I think this game is not fair because it's more even products in multiplying. I was even and I got 11 points and partner that was odd he got only 5." He wasn't the only one who realized that the game would be very unfair to Player Two. Desirae wrote, "I think that this game is not fair because when I did this experiment player 1 had 8 point and player 2 had none. . . . I would like to be number 1 because I want to see how it feel to be the winner."

Did these students learn what it means for a game to be fair? Maybe not completely. But they were exposed to an experiment that forced them to think about what this means. And with additional probability activities (perhaps spinners that have varied sizes or cubes in bags with different amounts of certain colors in each), they will get practice with other mathematical concepts while learning about the idea of fairness.

Figure 1–2 *Students collaborating on their conclusions after playing the game*

Figure 1–3 *Students recording conclusions after playing the game*

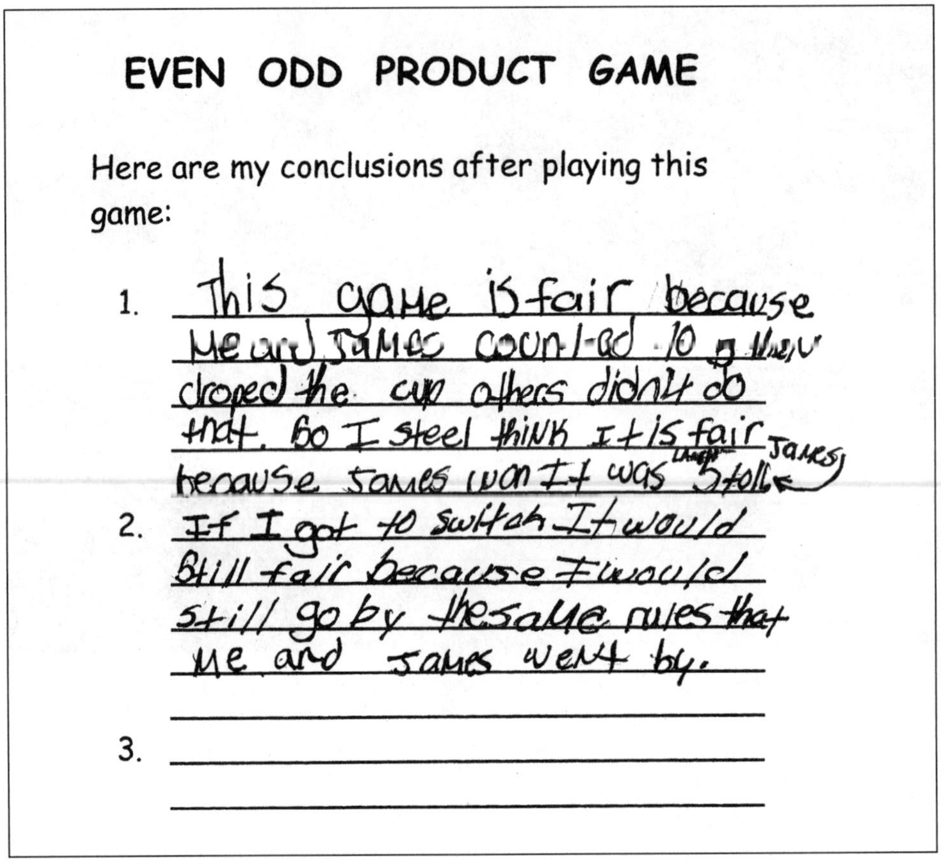

EVEN ODD PRODUCT GAME

Here are my conclusions after playing this game:

1. This game is fair because me and James counted 10 m then droped the cup others didn't do that. So I steel think it is fair because James won it was 3 toll James.

2. If I got to switch It would Still fair because I would still go by the same rules that me and James went by.

3. _____

Figure 1–4 *Lanell concluded that fairness is determined by playing by the rules.*

As practitioners, we quickly realize the role of content connections in effective and efficient planning for the implementation of a mathematics curriculum. Once we adjust to a routine practice of identifying potential connections that exist among content areas in mathematics, some of the pressures of "not enough time" are relieved. When we target multiple concepts within a single lesson and plan for such connections, we maximize the learning potential and enable students to witness the global utility of mathematics.

Imagine for a moment that you are traveling from your home to a specific destination, taking the one and only route you know. Encountering a road block could leave you lost and feeling helpless. You may be somewhat hesitant to explore alternative routes if you are in unfamiliar territory. This sometimes happens with students in mathematics class. It is our obligation as teachers to equip students with the confidence and means to feel comfortable about taking an alternative route. Building and strengthening connections provides alternative routes to understand problems and reach solutions. Teaching students to mimic a set of procedures will not serve him or her well. Students do reach stumbling points as they approach mathematics problems so by facilitating connections among mathematics concepts and skills we provide them with a broader view of mathematics, better enabling them to understand and navigate through the content, and feeling equipped with options when facing challenges.

Lessons intentionally planned to highlight connections are more meaningful to students and offer opportunities to build upon and exercise mathematical power.

EVEN ODD PRODUCT GAME

Here are my conclusions after playing this game:

1. I think this game is fair because there whany a even chanse to get even or odd numders there is 3 odd numders on the dice, and 3 even.

2. This giltme is not fair if I was a 2 because when Veroniona gaid there was more even on the Multiplication Chart.

3. To win at this game you need to be even. When you are odd there is less odds and more evens on the multiplication chart. Even will win!!

Figure 1–5 *As Anthony reasons through, he amends his conclusion.*

These learning experiences move beyond isolated skills and are often achieved in problem-solving scenarios, scenarios designed to enhance the inherent connections that exist among the categories of mathematics.

The following task illustrates such connections, primarily among the content areas of measurement and number and operations. When introducing this task, Ms. Gallo provides an immediate "hook" for students by displaying five empty boxes of various sizes. These are covered in white or brown paper so that students don't know what the content of each box has been. Such boxes could include an empty game or puzzle box, an old shoe box, a jewelry box, a cereal box, and a crayon box. Ms. Gallo poses the following problem to students:

Wrappings and Ribbons

Have you ever bought a special gift for a friend? Maybe it was for their birthday, or for a special holiday?

How much wrapping paper and ribbon would you need to wrap these gifts? How much would it cost to purchase the correct amount of paper and ribbon?

Ms. Gallo's problem is authentic in that students are likely to encounter such a situation in their lives. And students appear to be immediately intrigued by the boxes.

EVEN ODD PRODUCT GAME

Here are my conclusions after playing this game:

1. I think that this game is not fair because when I did this experiment player 1 had 8 point and player 2 had hade. I also think this is not fair because even had more than player one.

2. I would like to be number 1 because I want to see how it feel to be the winner. I would also like to be player one because I want to win the other player.

3. To win at this game you need to have dice. You also need to make this game even so that the other player can have the same chance of winning this game.

Figure 1-6 *Desirae suggests changes to make the game fair.*

The task is quite open-ended and requires that students think about how to begin to solve this problem. This is a great opportunity for Ms. Gallo to ask students to generate questions that must be answered before they can proceed. The following questions are then generated by this class, and posted on chart paper:

- How much paper is on a roll of wrapping paper?

- How long is a roll of ribbon?

- What is the price of a roll of wrapping paper?

- How much does a roll of ribbon cost?

- How big are the different boxes?

At this point, Ms. Gallo reveals a roll of gift wrap, a roll of ribbon, and the receipt for the two items. The amount of gift wrap and ribbon are listed on each label and the receipt indicates the cost. The response to each question is then written. Next, Ms. Gallo asks students to consider the steps they need to take to solve the problem.

She gives them time to think on their own for thirty seconds and then follows with small-group discussion time. Following this reflection and discussion, several students share possible next steps:

STUDENT: We need to measure the boxes to figure out how much stuff to use.
STUDENT: You mean measure around the box, like the paper and ribbon will be.
STUDENT: Then you tell the price.
TEACHER: How would measuring the boxes help to determine the price?
STUDENT: If we add all the measurements we can figure out the price.

At this point, Ms. Gallo distributes a box and inch tape measures to small groups of students. Each group works for several minutes to determine the required length of paper and ribbon for their specific box. The requested lengths are recorded on a class table (see Figure 1–7).

Then Ms. Gallo rewords the original question, "How many rolls of wrapping paper and how many rolls of ribbon are needed?" It becomes apparent to the students that their recorded lengths are in inches, and the labels on the rolls are displayed in feet and yards. The students quickly realize that they need to convert the measurements to a common unit in order to find the total length of gift wrap and ribbon for all of the packages.

This provided a rationale for students to recall the conversions among customary units of linear measure, and complete the calculations in order to compare the

**Wrappings and Ribbons
Purchase Information**

Materials	Dimensions	Price
Roll of Gift Wrap	2.5' x 6'	$4.35
Roll of Ribbon	8 yards	$1.35

Class Quantities

Gift Box	Gift Wrap Needed	Ribbon Needed
Box A	37"	78"
Box B	18"	47"
Box C	52"	125.5"
Box D	21"	50"
Box E	10"	34"
Totals	138"	334.5"

Figure 1-7 *Class table of requested lengths of ribbon and paper*

numeric values. Juan's work illustrates his use of division and multiplication in order to make the comparisons (see Figure 1–8).

Additionally, Juan uses addition to find the total cost. Juan goes on to record his use of measurement (length), division, multiplication, money, tables, estimation, and conversions in completing this task. Upon completion of the list of concepts he says, "Boy, I know a lot about math!" Juan's statement is indicative of an empowered learner.

Finally, Ms. Gallo cuts and distributes lengths of paper (from a roll of graph paper) and yarn to the exact lengths originally requested by each group. She instructs the students to confirm their measurements and calculations by using these materials to wrap the gifts. Excitement fills the room as small groups work eagerly to completely cover the box with paper and decorate it with a bow made of yarn. The students smile with satisfaction. Ms. Gallo grins with the knowledge that this single experience allowed students to understand and appreciate the connections among the content areas of mathematics.

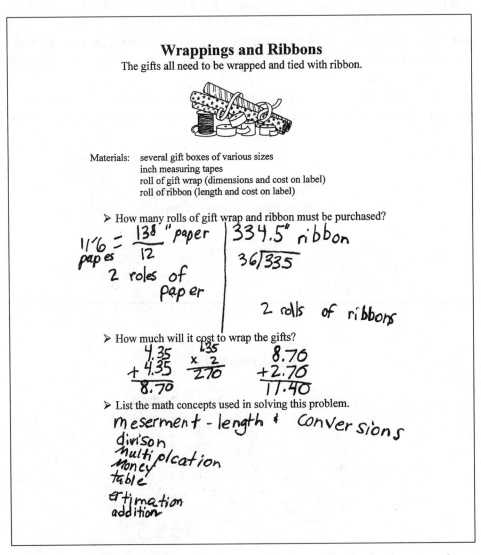

Figure 1–8 *Juan's work illustrates his use of division and multiplication in order to make comparisons.*

The mathematics category of measurement is extremely comprehensive. So much so, that it is often difficult for students to fully visualize how all of the attributes, tools, and units of measurement fit together and relate to one another. Students must differentiate between such attributes as linear measure, capacity, time, area, perimeter, volume, weight, mass, temperature, and angle measure. The additional task of recalling appropriate tools used to measure each attribute and distinguishing between unit systems can be confusing. We have found that an ongoing visual display in the classroom, like the one shown in Figure 1–9, can offer students the aid they need to categorize the ideas of measurement.

MEASUREMENT

What Attribute?	What Tools?	What Units?	
		Customary	Metric
length perimeter	ruler yardstick meter stick trundle wheel tape measure	inches feet yards miles	millimeters centimeters decimeters meters kilometer
weight	scale	ounces pounds tons	grams kilograms
capacity	measuring cups	cups pints quarts gallons	milliliters liters
time	clock sundial calendar	seconds hours days weeks months years decades	
angles	protractors squares	degrees	
temperature	thermometer	Fahrenheit degrees	Celsius degrees
area	ruler yardstick meter stick inch tiles trundle wheel	sq inches sq feet sq yards sq miles acres	sq millimeters sq centimeters sq decimeters sq kilometers

*Continue adding to the display throughout the year

Figure 1–9 *Measurement*

The organizer begins with a big idea within measurement and then lists tools and units within that big idea. This display would serve well as a classroom bulletin board. It should be be updated as the year progresses and more forms of measurement are addressed in the curriculum.

CLASSROOM-TESTED TIP

We often provide opportunities for students to share their strategies when solving problems. While this is an invaluable practice, it can sometimes be difficult for students to maintain their attention while others are verbally sharing with the class. Even students who appear to be listening, by sitting quietly and looking at the speaker, may not be hearing and reflecting on the discourse taking place. One technique to engage students in active listening is to give a purpose for listening. We often say, "While Susan is sharing her strategy, I would like you to think about two things:

1. Do I understand and agree with her thinking?

2. Did I do it the same way, or do I have a different strategy?"

The prompt provides a specific purpose for listening and elicits further discourse among students. We think these are obvious questions to consider whenever we listen to a speaker, but students need to learn such skills through our modeling. For this reason, it is important to state these questions in the first person. Students then begin the practice of asking these questions of themselves, without prompting from the teacher.

Questions for Discussion

1. What are the benefits of using tasks that highlight connections among many mathematics content areas?

2. What impact does student recognition of the mathematics connections have on student learning, attitude, and achievement?

3. What role does questioning play in fostering the ability to identify connections in mathematics?

4. How might the lessons in this chapter be adapted to meet the needs of your students?

CHAPTER 2

Mathematical Ideas Interconnect and Build Upon One Another

These connections help students see mathematics as a unified body of knowledge rather than a set of complex and disjoint concepts, procedures, and processes.

—National Council of Teachers of Mathematics,
Principles and Standards for School Mathematics

Importance for Student Learning

Mr. Moran's third-grade class had been introduced to the big ideas about multiplication and were now immersed in this study. For several days, students explored the use of different strategies as they solved a variety of problems that had been given to them. These problems were helping them build a clear understanding of what it meant to multiply, and how to represent multiplication in various ways. A week had passed and Mr. Moran displayed the following problem, at the front of the room, for his students to solve.

> **Juan went to the store and bought a bag of 12 candies. The candies included equal amounts of 4 different flavors. How many candies were there of each flavor?**

Students were given a minute to think about this problem. Then Mr. Moran asked for volunteers to share their solution. Michael raised his hand and proudly responded "48." Mr. Moran was puzzled. Michael was very confident and successful in his mathematical abilities, yet on this problem his answer was incorrect.

Mr. Moran questioned, "What makes you think that 48 is the answer?"

Michael explained, "Twelve times 4 equals 48."

"Yes," replied Mr. Moran, "that is true, but how do you know that 48 is the answer to this problem?"

Michael responded, "Because we are doing multiplication, so I multiplied the two numbers."

Mr. Moran is not the first teacher to hear this form of logic from a student. Students assume that if they have been learning about multiplication then any problem that they'll be given must be a multiplication problem. Michael shared this conclusion with his teacher, but it is likely that others in the class were thinking the same thing.

We can remember textbooks where the only problems that were given were at the end of the chapter. And if the chapter covered multiplication, the problems would all use multiplication as well. Why is it that we didn't realize this? Those problems at the end of the chapter always caused us difficulty.

Unfortunately, these assumptions are typical of many students. Mathematics is often viewed as a series of isolated skills to work through; the intent is to finish one unit, only to then move on and complete yet another new and disconnected unit of study. All too often learners fail to recognize that the ideas are interrelated and build upon one another to produce a network of connected concepts and patterns, holistically known as *mathematics*. Maybe this is something we need to help them with. Maybe, if we point out how concepts are related or we mention that we'll be using this new skill when we're learning something later in the year our students won't be as prone to see mathematics in this way.

This compartmentalized perspective limits Michael, and other students, to a shallow perception of the complexity and interconnectedness of mathematics. Is it useful for Michael to know how to multiply if he does not know when to multiply? Mr. Moran presented the problem to the class with the hope that his students would apply their conceptual understanding of multiplication to a division situation. But, it was his next step that was crucial in facilitating Michael's ability to construct such a connection.

Mr. Moran asked, "How many total candies are there in this story?"

Michael reread the problem and quickly responded with a quiet, but somewhat confused, "It says 12, so it can't be 48."

After several seconds of reflection, Michael shouted out, "Oh, I get it! There are 12 candies in four different colors, so 4 times something equals 12. It's 3! There are 3 of each flavor!" (Do you feel Michael's pride? Wasn't this worth the time spent in questioning?)

Michael's response had paved the way for Mr. Moran to highlight the connection between multiplication and division; allowing students to forge and travel another of the many paths that interconnect the content areas of mathematics. Michael was able to build upon his understanding of multiplication and related facts to solve the division problem. He didn't even have to know that he was doing division to figure this out. He just had to reason and use what he had already made sense of to figure out the answer to this new situation.

The dialogue between Mr. Moran and Michael illustrates the significance and benefit when educators recognize that mathematical ideas are interwoven. The story of Juan and his candy of four flavors includes mathematical ideas of multiplication, division, and algebra. These categories also relate to the bigger idea of equivalence, which is a major focus for this grade. The more students experience these connections, in a variety of tasks and activities, the stronger the foundation of understanding.

The Teacher's Role

Mr. Moran played a vital role in the previously described scenario. He could have told Michael that his answer was incorrect and that he needed to think harder about what the answer might be. He could have called on another student who he thought had the correct answer and ended the line of questioning entirely. But, he didn't. He chose to take the time to explore Michael's thinking in greater depth, to determine what it is that Michael had been thinking about. His questions helped to diagnose a common misconception, that learning about multiplication must mean that the problems we're being given are multiplication problems. His open-ended and specific questions prompted Michael to communicate his thinking and even make sense out of his initial response. Mr. Moran became the perfect facilitator, illustrating the role of the teacher in helping students "understand how mathematical ideas interconnect and build on one another to produce a coherent whole" (NCTM 2000).

Describing our role in fostering the recognition of the connected nature of mathematics begins with the selection of the tasks we choose for students. These tasks should include opportunities for students to engage in and explore complex and sophisticated mathematical ideas. Mr. Moran chose a problem beyond the typical scope of multiplication structures and provided a more complex look at the connections between multiplication and division. By keeping the numbers reasonable he allowed students, who were just learning about multiplication, to make sense out of a different scenario. This problem offered a rationale to explore ideas of division and a reason to further examine the notion that division is the inverse operation of multiplication.

Once a task or problem has been selected and offered to students, our role becomes one of an observer and questioner. At first we need to step back and watch while students struggle (somewhat) with a challenging problem. Once they have had some time to think about the problem at hand it is up to us to begin asking questions that probe their thinking. The questions we ask enable students to recall what they already know and understand, and challenge them to apply this knowledge to a new situation. Questions often serve as encouragement for students to communicate their thoughts, explore alternative strategies, and justify responses.

Mr. Moran responded to Michael's incorrect answer with a series of questions. He never told Michael his answer was incorrect. Instead, he led Michael through several inquiries that challenged him to justify his response. Mr. Moran's prompts to Michael were all in question format. They included:

- "How many total candies are there in the story?"

- "What makes you think that 48 is the answer?"

- "Yes, but how do you know that 48 is the answer to this problem?"

Michael was not embarrassed when he was unable to justify his response. He was just confused, since mathematics usually made sense to him. So, given some time to reflect he made the connection between the problem and what he already understood about multiplication. Then he self-corrected. Michael never felt threatened, nor put on the spot. The questions were not judgmental in nature and were posed to focus Michael's attention and help him make a connection to what he'd been learning about.

What might be a good follow-up question? Mr. Moran could ask a "what-if?" to further determine whether Michael really understood the connection he'd just made. He might ask, "What if there were six colors instead of four? Then how many candies of each color would there be?"

This would allow Mr. Moran to further clarify the concept with another example for Michael and for the rest of the class. These exchanges of questions and answers don't take a terribly long period of time to make. Other students could surely be called on to offer their own interpretation of the problem or follow-up questions. As long as the connections and students' understanding are the focus of the lesson, the questions that are asked play an important part in the lesson.

Questioning is a powerful instructional tool. Posing questions keeps learners engaged and accountable during instruction, and provides valuable information regarding student understanding. Asking questions directs the power to the learner. Michael did all of the mathematics, not Mr. Moran.

Sometimes during instruction teachers end up modeling for students or telling students much of the mathematics that they want students to learn. Students observe and then mimic what they've seen. But when we view our role as a facilitator and continue to prompt student learning with questions, the knowledge is constructed within the student, it is not merely replicated. This is a more reflective and often more difficult manner of teaching. And, it certainly takes planning and an analysis of what's to be taught. But, if true understanding is at the heart of what we're doing, this way of teaching provides students so many more opportunities for understanding to occur.

We often ask ourselves the following question when we are teaching students, "Who is doing more mathematics, me or the students?" If we're doing most of the work, the writing, the telling, the modeling, the drawing, then our students are just watching and waiting. We want them to be thinking, doing, and discussing. This seems to happen best if we ask more and tell less.

CLASSROOM-TESTED TIP

We often teach students to read a math problem and first identify the question being asked. This is an important skill so that students are able to answer the question correctly. Additionally, the question provides focus and direction in reaching a solution. The question determines how the information will be manipulated or calculated to get the answer. Consider for a moment what would happen if a problem was presented to the class minus the question. Let's use Mr. Moran's problem as an example:

Juan went to the store and bought a bag of 12 candies. The candies included equal amounts of 4 different flavors.

By revealing the situation first (without the question), students have time to comprehend the scenario and do not feel compelled to quickly jump to a strategy or solution. One idea is to cover the question, recorded on chart paper, with a separate piece of paper so that after some discussion, the question can easily be exposed. While the question is concealed, the class can pause to consider the problem, identify what they already know, and truly grasp the context before working toward a solution. This also provides time for students to reflect on similar situations in their own lives, and make connections to other problems or contexts.

Additionally, we must allow and assist students in exploring mathematical connections by having them describe the strategies that they use to reach a solution to a problem. Of course this is facilitated, in part, by the tasks we choose and the questions we pose. But, it is also accomplished by the materials and the manipulatives we select for a lesson, as well as the time we allot for students to share strategies with the class.

Here's an example of how the use of a specific material provided students an opportunity to make sense out of a previous understanding and then use it to solve a more challenging problem. Mrs. Brady, a third-grade teacher, decided to provide her students with a hundreds chart while they counted coins. Having used this in the past to look at skip counting, her students easily applied their knowledge of counting by fives and tens to counting pennies, nickels, dimes, and quarters. The hundreds chart served as a visual cue when changing units while skip counting. As her students explained how they had used this chart, it became clear that they had realized that it was easier to begin with the larger units (quarters), and then count the smaller units (pennies).

Students in Mr. Burns' class often used measuring tapes in place of number lines for locating specific values. This then enabled students to recognize the numerals on an analog clock as an arrangement of two number lines being read simultaneously—the hour numerals and the minutes numerals. This connection was reinforced when Mr. Burns bent the measuring tapes to form circles resembling an analog clock.

In another classroom, Ms. Davidson used a multiplication chart made of grid paper so students could explore the connection between the multiplication table and the dimensions and area of a rectangle.

In each of these examples, classroom teachers were making purposeful choices about the materials they were using as they planned for instruction. We must consider the power and utility of the materials we choose, and use them flexibly and appropriately so students build on their levels of understanding and grasp a more inclusive and intertwined view of mathematics.

We must also encourage students to describe how they are using the materials. Such math discourse may occur from teacher to student, student to teacher, and student to student. Mr. Samuels sets aside time during every math lesson for students to share their ideas and strategies within small groups or with the entire class. He recalls his class and explains,

> I know it takes a lot of time, but it is worth it! In the process of articulating ideas, I have witnessed Lana's pride in sharing a correct answer, Sarah's reflection as she recognizes an error and corrects the mistake without interjection from me, Tommy's relief after listening to Alex's ideas and now diving into a problem he felt was too difficult, and Cerina's excitement when she shared a strategy different from all of the others. These moments all took place when students had the chance to communicate their ideas with peers. I am saddened to think of all of the missed opportunities if I chose not to take time each day for students to describe their mathematics processes. Sharing helps them relate to one another and to the mathematics.

Connecting Ideas of Area

A fifth-grade class is exploring the concept of *area*. Students were introduced to area in earlier grades where they measured the area of figures on a grid. These skills were later expanded to more formulized equations, such as using length times width to determine the area of a rectangle. Mrs. Cohen presented the following task (see Which Is the Best Pizza Value? in the Mathematical Ideas Interconnect and Build Upon One Another section of the CD) to students to advance their understanding of area:

> *Is one pizza a better value over the others?*
>
> **A local pizza shop sells all pies for the same low price of $5.99. However, they offer the pizzas in a variety of shapes. Based on the pizza models provided, is one pizza a better value than the others?**

Small groups of three to four students received rulers, one-inch tiles, one-inch grid paper, pizza models (see Figure 2–1), calculators, scissors, and measuring tapes.

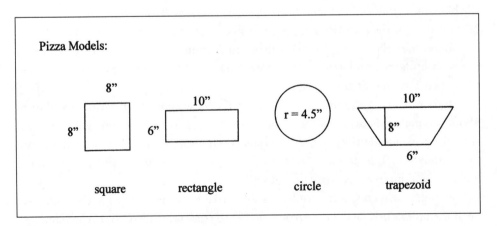

Figure 2–1 *Pizza models for best pizza deal activity*

The materials for each group were housed in a pizza box that was donated by a local pizza shop. Mrs. Cohen let students read the problem and describe what is meant by "a better value." Sonja summed it up well when she said, "It's like getting the most for your money." The students eagerly opened their pizza boxes and explored the models. Some of their observations are captured here:

STUDENT: I think the circle is the better value.
TEACHER: Why do you think so?
STUDENT: I don't know, it just looks bigger.
TEACHER: Think about how you could verify your estimate. Talk it over with your group.
STUDENT: What shape is this [pointing to the trapezoid]?
STUDENT: It is a trapezoid. Remember the red piece in the pattern blocks?
STUDENT: The trapezoid looks like it is the same size as the square.
TEACHER: How did you compare the two shapes?
STUDENT: If I overlap the two shapes, I could cut the little corners off at the bottom and put them at the top, and it would be the square.
TEACHER: You may use the scissors to cut the models if you like.

Mrs. Cohen circulated throughout the room, listening to the group conversations, observing student strategies, and posing questions. She provided time for students to make conjectures and recall prior knowledge that could then be applied to this new situation. Hannah immediately began with the square. She started by placing tiles on the model to cover the entire surface. She counted the tiles one by one and recorded 64 square inches on her paper. Luis, from another group, also chose the tiles, but only did one row of tiles horizontally across the top of the square, and another row vertically along the side of the square. He counted to eight for both measures, recalled that 8×8 equaled 64, and recorded the information on his sheet. A third strategy was revealed by Veronica. She measured one side of the square and promptly recorded 64 in² on her page. When Mrs. Cohen asked why she did so, she explained "the area of a rectangle is length times width and since this is a square, I only had to measure one side." Mrs. Cohen allowed Hannah, Luis, and Veronica to share their strategies with the class in the same sequence as described here. She felt that this sequence illustrated for students how the ideas connect and built upon one another from a concrete level to a more abstract calculation of the area of a square.

Similar strategies were used by different students in the class to find the area of the rectangle. However, Mrs. Cohen noticed that more students, including Hannah and Luis, abandoned the tiles (the method they used to find the area of the square), and used the length times width formula shared by Veronica when tackling the rectangular pizza model. She attributed this shift to the class' discussion of the strategies used with the square. The students saw the connection between the square and the rectangle, and applied the formula when finding the area.

Madyson was a member of Eva's group, and Mrs. Cohen was curious to see if these students would explore her earlier speculation that the trapezoid could be transformed into a square. She listened as she heard Jose ask whether they could use the length times width formula for finding out the trapezoid's area. Richard pointed out to Jose that a square had the same length on top and on bottom and that the "triangles on the ends would have to come off for the formula to work." Mrs. Cohen watched as Eva used the ruler to measure the height of the trapezoid and said, "Yes, but it won't be a square because the height is eight inches and the top is only six inches."

Here is where the students' conversation got interesting.

STUDENT: But the bottom is ten inches, so could we use some of that?

STUDENT (*after a moment*): We could cut the triangle off the end at two inches and put it on the other side to make a square.

The other students considered this suggestion and decided to try out Eva's idea.

"Now this pizza is exactly the same as the square pizza, 64 square inches," exclaimed Jose. Mrs. Cohen asked Jose which would be the better value. He explained that they were the same value because the area was now the same. When Jose said "the area is now the same" Mrs. Cohen became concerned that Jose might think that the area of the trapezoid pizza changed when the pieces were cut and reconfigured. She quickly took another trapezoid model, showed it to Jose and asked him what the area would be. He looked at it and thought for several seconds. Then he explained that if he could cut off the end, again, and tape it to the other side it would be 64 square inches. "What if I didn't cut it off and tape it to the other side?" Mrs. Cohen asked. Jose looked confused.

Figure 2–2 *Eva transforming the trapezoid into a square*

Mrs. Cohen continued with her questions, "If this were a real pizza and I cut the end off and placed it on the other side, would I still have the same amount of pizza?"

"Oh yeah," said Jose, "We'd still have all of the pizza. We just moved it around a little." Mrs. Cohen, assured that Jose really does understand the original quantity of pizza was unchanged by the manipulation, moved to observe another group as they worked on this problem.

The final pizza model in the box was a circle. Mrs. Cohen knew that this pizza model would offer the greatest challenge for students since they had done very little with circles, circumference, diameter, or area with this plane figure. As she moved from one group to another, she noted that one group was finding an approximate area by covering the model with square tiles. These students tried to compensate for the misfit of the square tiles on the round figure by counting the total tiles and adding a few more to the total to account for additional spaces. As she watched this group she noticed that Julio was using a piece of grid paper. Finding the tiles troublesome to use, he traced the circle onto this grid paper.

Julio then combined pieces on the square grid and counted these squares. He arrived at an estimated area of 62 square inches.

To Mrs. Cohen's surprise, she observed Nate writing πr^2 on the circular pizza model. When she asked him about this he explained that it was the formula for finding the area of a circle. "How do you know this?" Mrs. Cohen asked him. His reply was that his older sister had taught this to him. Nate's answer for the area of the

Figure 2–3 *Julio's strategy for finding the area of a circle*

circle was 63.62 in^2. As Mrs. Cohen continued talking with him he stated that π was 3.14. He said, "I measured the radius of the circle and it's 4.5 inches." Mrs. Cohen asked him how he knew that π equaled 3.14. "I don't know," he replied, "but it works—see." This fifth grader understood that the radius was half of the diameter of a circle. He also knew how to square the radius and he was able to multiply the product times pi. What he did not know, however, was what pi represented, and why the formula worked.

Mrs. Cohen had to determine how to have him share what he knew, since the range of abilities in this class was vast. Here was a class where some students were covering surfaces with square tiles and then counting these tiles, one-by-one, while another student was using the formula πr^2 to determine the area. In many classes this is the sort of range that exists, because by the time a student gets into fifth grade there are a multitude of factors that influence their understanding of mathematics concepts.

Mrs. Cohen decided that a good way of helping students understand Nate's strategy was to demonstrate how to transform a circle into a rectangle. She made this decision based on the prior knowledge demonstrated by this class. This particular class was very comfortable using strategies to find the area of a rectangle and even manipulated the trapezoid to fit the definition of the rectangle. So she decided to take the same approach with the circle. Her hope was that students would make the connection and further their understanding of area of different shapes.

She felt that Julio would benefit because he was seeking a more accurate calculation, rather than simply an estimate with the tiles. The demonstration would also offer Nate some insight into why the formula for the circle worked. Mrs. Cohen gathered the class together on the floor and began with the circle pizza model. She cut the circle in half (through the diameter) and was left with two semicircles. Next, she overlapped the semicircles and began making pielike wedges by cutting from the center point toward the outside, stopping just before reaching the edge. Mrs. Cohen then separated the two semicircles, fanned them out, and merged the pieces together to form a rectangular shape (see Figure 2–4). The students appeared amazed and the classroom discourse continued.

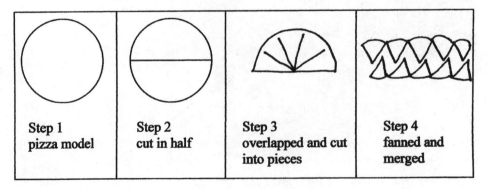

Figure 2–4 *Steps to transform the trapezoid into a square*

STUDENT: Wow, when you did that you made a rectangle.

TEACHER: And, how do you find the area of a rectangle?

STUDENT: It's just length times width.

TEACHER: So, what is the length and the width of this rectangle, which was transformed from a circle?

STUDENT: The width is the radius of the circle.

TEACHER: What about the length?

STUDENT: The length is the perimeter.

TEACHER: (*following up*) But, what is the perimeter of a circle called?

STUDENT: I mean it's the circumference. The perimeter of the circle is the circle's circumference.

Here is where Mrs. Cohen did some summarizing (for any student who hadn't been following this line of questioning as closely).

TEACHER: So, the length is the circumference?

STUDENT: No, not the whole length, only half of it.

TEACHER: Why only half of it is the length?

STUDENT: Because the length is only the top half of the circumference. The other half is the length on the bottom of the rectangle.

TEACHER (*to the group*): So, what is our equation for finding the area of this circle? (*The class remained quiet for several seconds.*)

STUDENT: Area equals radius times half of the circumference.

TEACHER: OK, then how will we find these measurements?

STUDENT: The radius is four and a half.

TEACHER: How can we find the circumference?

STUDENT: We could use the measuring tape that's in our pizza box. It bends, so we can put it around the whole circle.

Using the class-constructed formula, the students calculated that the area of the circle was 63 square inches. Mrs. Cohen asked the class to compare this with Julio's original response of 62 square inches and Nate's answer of 63.62 square inches. The students concluded that Julio's answer was an estimate—and a pretty good one. And they all felt that the other answers were very close. Everyone agreed that the area of the circular pizza was about 63 square inches. The students recorded the pizza dimensions (see Figure 2–5) and the class concluded that the square and trapezoid pizzas were the better value, but the circle was very close.

Is this real-life mathematics? It certainly is! And the students also talked about the fact that a customer who did not like crust would find that the circular pizza was the better choice because the area was close but the perimeter was four inches shorter. The extension to this problem was in the home assignment that Mrs. Cohen gave to her students. She challenged them to construct a pizza with about the same area as the models used in the lesson. But (and here was the challenge) this pizza had to have a different shape than a rectangle, trapezoid, or circle. Each student got one-inch grid paper and excitedly put this away as they shared with friends what they were going to try to do.

Is one pizza a better value over the others?

➤ Which pizza is the better value? A and D

Ⓐ
c= ½ c x r
l x w
180
x 6
480 sq in
144.5 = 63

Pizza Specifics

Pizza	Dimensions	Area	Perimeter
A ▢	8 X 8	64 sq in	32 in.
B ▭	6 X 10	60 sq in	32 in.
C ◯	4 ½	63 sq. in.	28 in.
D ▱	8 6 10	64 sq in.	32 in.

➤ If you especially love crust, is any one pizza a better choice? A, B and D

➤ Design a pizza of a different shape with a similar value.

Figure 2–5 *Eva's recording sheet*

Did this lesson illustrate the idea that mathematics concepts build upon one another? It really did. And, even if some students didn't quite "get" the idea of how to make sense out of finding the area of a circle, they've now been exposed to this in an experiential way. When it's presented again, as it will be in sixth grade, they will have this prior experience to draw on.

These students were able to extend their knowledge of measurement from finding the area of a rectangle to the next level of finding the area of trapezoids and circles. Students were able to see the connection among these shapes and use what they knew about rectangles to find the area of more complex figures. Mrs. Cohen purposefully chose these specific shapes in order to facilitate such connections.

If you were to duplicate this activity in your own classroom, you might want to limit the set of pizza models provided to students. In fact, the versatility in choosing which models to provide serves as a means for differentiating instruction. For third graders, limiting the set to squares and rectangles seems reasonable. Fourth graders may tackle the addition of the trapezoid, while fifth graders could explore with all four models. The benefit is that you can adjust the level of difficulty by deciding which models to include. This flexibility is possible because the pizza models are part of the materials list, and are not included in the context of the problem. The remaining materials are important in that they provide students with a choice as to the strategies they might use in reaching their solution.

Developing Multiplicative Reasoning

Multiplicative reasoning is a major theme in mathematics for students in the intermediate grades. This theme includes knowledge of multiplication and division skills, as well as student analysis of situations in which multiplication and division serve as an operation for reaching a solution. Recognition and discussion of the connections that exist within the structures of multiplication and division empower learners to build a strong foundation for proportional reasoning in middle school (NCTM 2000). The concepts and structures of multiplication must be developed and fostered in third grade and continue through fifth grade.

Let's examine some tasks and student work samples collected throughout the year in Ms. Lucas' third-grade class. These samples highlight some key ideas of multiplication. The first is a lesson entitled Popcorn Sales (also in the Mathematical Ideas Interconnect and Build Upon One Another section on the CD). Ms. Lucas began this lesson by asking her students whether any of them belonged to girl scouts, boy scouts, or a girls or boys club. Very few students raised their hands. So, Ms. Lucas knew that she needed these "hand raisers" to share what belonging to a girls or boys club meant. She asked them to explain what sorts of activities they did. Once it was clear that the entire class knew that fundraising was something that every organization seemed to do, she showed her students the following problem (which was also written on their paper):

Steven sold 9 cases of popcorn for scouts. Each case held 6 boxes of popcorn. How many boxes of popcorn did he sell?

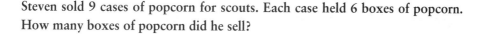

Ms. Lucas provided plenty of blank space on the sheet to offer students flexibility in choosing a strategy. Minh began by drawing nine boxes and labeled each with the number six. He then wrote the equation to represent the repeated addition of six, nine times. Minh hesitated on the total so he went back and drew six tally marks in each box and counted the tallies one-by-one until he reached fifty-four. In doing this he demonstrated his understanding that multiplication is repeated addition and he drew a picture to illustrate this connection (see Figure 2–6).

Kathryn used skip counting to solve this problem. Initially, she also drew nine boxes labeled with the number six to represent the cases of popcorn. She then went back and crossed out each box as she counted by sixes until she reached fifty-four as her answer. Finally, Kathryn wrote the multiplication equation to describe the situation. She was able to build upon the idea of repeated sets by instituting a skip counting strategy. Kathryn then connected both skills to a multiplication equation (see Figure 2–7).

Later in the school year, this same third-grade class began exploring the idea of *area*. Ms. Lucas presented a task called Rectangle Constructions to her students (see

Figure 2–6 *Minh's connection between repeated addition and multiplication*

the Mathematical Ideas Interconnect and Build Upon One Another section on the CD). Students were to use grid paper to construct as many different rectangles as they could, all having an area of 24 square units. They were asked to answer the following problem:

How many different rectangles can you create with an area of 24 square units? What strategy did you use to create the rectangles?

Counters and grid paper were made available for student use. Ms. Lucas was curious to see how the students would apply their knowledge of multiplication to the solving of this new problem. Ronald's strategy was to gather twenty-four counters and arrange them in arrays. If the array was complete (three rows of eight, for example), he recorded the arrangement on the grid paper. If one of the rows on the array was incomplete, Ronald would try again with a different arrangement. Ms. Lucas noticed that Ronald wrote that he had found three rectangles with an area of 24 square units, yet he had four arrays recorded on his grid paper (see Figure 2–8).

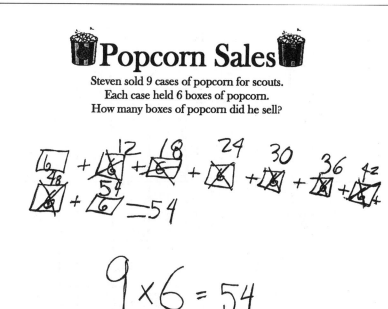

Figure 2–7 *Kathryn's connection between skip counting and a multiplication equation*

Rectangle Constructions

Use the grid paper to construct as many different rectangles with an area of 24 square units as possible.

How many different rectangles can you create with an area of 24 square units?

I found 3.

What strategy did you use to create the rectangles?

I used 24 chips. I put them in rows and I looked to see if they where even, colrd on the grid. They are arays.

Figure 2–8 12×2 and 2×12 are not unique arrays for the product 24.

(continues)

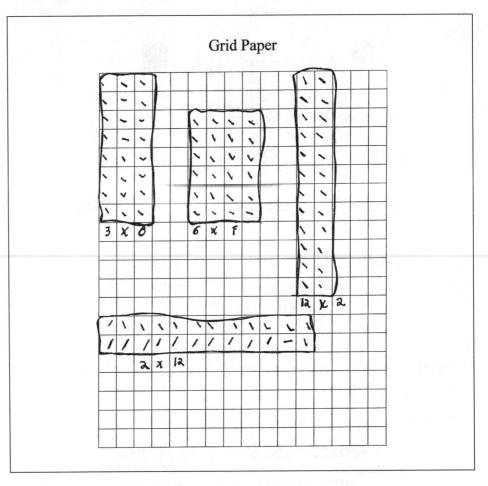

Figure 2–8 *Continued*

He explained to Ms. Lucas that a "2 × 12 array is the same as a 12 × 2 array be-cause you just turn it." Ronald demonstrated his understanding that the arrays were congruent and a rotation did not make it a unique array, so it was not counted in his total.

CLASSROOM-TESTED TIP

Manipulatives are a powerful resource in the mathematics classroom. They provide concrete and visual representations so students may better grasp new concepts and ideas. However, sometimes it is beneficial to provide too few ma-terials. There are situations in which limiting the quantity of a particular ma-terial can encourage students to attain a higher level of understanding. Here is an example. John was using one-inch tiles to determine the area of a ten-inch by six-inch rectangle. He began to cover the rectangle with one-inch tiles when he realized that he didn't have enough to cover the entire figure. John called over to Mrs. Anderson and requested more tiles. Mrs. Anderson responded that she didn't have any additional tiles available. She asked John to consider another strategy to solve the problem. After some contemplation, John placed ten tiles across the top and six tiles along the side. He then did some mental calculations and recorded the area of the rectangle as 60 square inches. Mrs. Anderson returned, after circulating to other students, and questioned John about his answer. He responded by saying, "I just did a row across, then a column down and counted by tens, or I could say ten times six equals sixty." Mrs. Anderson was quite confident that if the tiles had been available, John would have placed them one-by-one over the entire shape, counting as he went along. He would have used a "less efficient" strategy if it hadn't been for the fact that he had fewer tiles than he needed. When the set of tiles was limited, John connected his knowledge of arrays, and length and width, to develop a more advanced strategy to find the area of the rectangle. Kelsey, another student in the class, folded her rectangle in half when confronted with the same limited number of tiles. She explained that she doubled her answer to find the area of the rectangle. Before giving her students this limited number of tiles, Mrs. Anderson knew that her students were ready to build upon their prior knowledge. She purposefully made the decision to give them fewer than they needed to cover the entire surface. Sometimes less is more. The key is to know your students and determine when they are ready to advance their understanding.

Cindy approached the problem very differently. She chose one number as a factor and then did mental computation to determine if there was another factor that would give a product of twenty-four. Her mental computation techniques included skip counting, and recall of basic multiplication facts. After finding a fact with a factor of 1, 2, 3, and 4, she assumed there would also be a set of factors with a product of 24 in which one of the factors was a 5. So, she drew it on the grid paper, but found it did not work (see Figure 2–9).

She even extended the grid paper in order to record the 1 × 24 array. The link that Cindy saw between products and the area of a rectangle made her more efficient as she worked on this task.

During a unit on probability, this same third-grade class worked out the solution to a combinations problem as another application of multiplication. The context of the task was to determine the total number of dessert choices given the choice of two ice cream flavors and four toppings (see We All Scream for Ice Cream! in the Mathematical Ideas Interconnect and Build Upon One Another section on the CD).

Tanya used an illustration resembling the set model for multiplication to represent the four toppings for each flavor of ice cream. Then she recorded 4 × 2 = 8 as the counting strategy (see Figure 2–10).

She did not begin the activity knowing that multiplication could be used to solve a combinations problem, but she did see her solution as a multiplication model and labeled it as such. A teacher might now wonder if Tanya would employ a multiplication

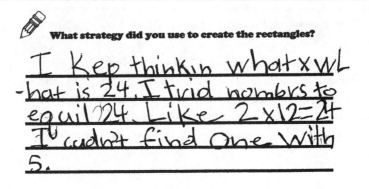

Rectangle Constructions
Use the grid paper to construct as many different rectangles
with an area of 24 square units as possible.

 **How many different rectangles can you create with
an area of 24 square units?**

4

 What strategy did you use to create the rectangles?

I Kep thinkin what x wL
-hat is 24. I trid nombrs to
equil 24. Like 2×12=24
I cudn't find One with
5.

Figure 2–9 *Cindy tries consecutive pairs of factors beginning with one.*

strategy sooner if presented with a similar combinations problem. This would be a logical next step for Ms. Lucas to pursue with the class.

Let's examine one final multiplication problem presented to Ms. Lucas' class. The problem was called Can Collections (see the Mathematical Ideas Interconnect and Build Upon One Another section on the CD). This is the problem she gave to her students:

> Maria and Stephen collected cans for a recycling project in their neighborhood. Maria collected 24 cans, while Stephen collected 8 cans. How many times more cans did Maria collect than Stephen? Draw a picture to show your solution.

Unlike with other problems, Ms. Lucas required the students to draw their solution because she felt it was the best way for her to determine their degree of understanding of this "comparison multiplication problem."

Ellen drew Stephen's 8 cans and then used the number 8 as a benchmark to create a geometric representation of Maria's cans. She showed that 24 is three times larger than 8. Ellen successfully applied a multiplication structure by connecting ideas of arrays, basic facts, and division (see Figure 2–11).

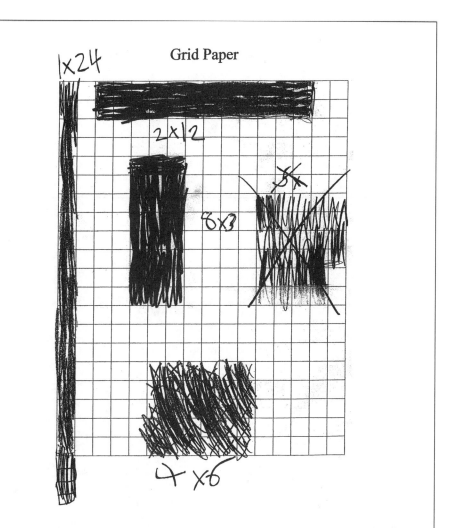

Figure 2–9 *Continued*

Ms. Lucas reinforced multiplication throughout the entire curriculum. She took advantage of multiple connections. Her third graders demonstrated the utility of multiplication and experienced the manner in which ideas build upon one another in a variety of contexts—groups, combinations, area, and comparisons. These experiences will enrich their foundation and prepare these students for more advanced structures and applications of multiplication in future grades.

It is our responsibility to help students feel empowered by the knowledge, and thus feel equipped to tackle any math problem. When instruction is based on the central ideas of mathematics and the connections that exist among those ideas, students develop a strong foundation from which to pull strategies and ideas. As educators we need to understand how the skills and concepts in mathematics build upon one another, and plan in a manner that illustrates such links for learners. Teachers must enable students to see mathematics not as a set of linear parallel paths and skills, but rather, as a network of interwoven themes and ideas.

We All Scream for Ice Cream!!

Oakwood Elementary School is holding an ice cream social. They offer a choice of chocolate ice cream <u>or</u> vanilla ice cream. You may also choose <u>one</u> of the following toppings:
- ✓ Sprinkles
- ✓ Marshmallow
- ✓ Cookie crumbs
- ✓ Strawberries

Shelly is trying to decide which ice cream and which topping to choose. She says, "There are so many choices, I cannot decide."

How many actual choices are there? Show your thinking with words, pictures, or numbers.

Figure 2–10 *Tanya's representation of the set model for multiplication*

CLASSROOM-TESTED TIP

Questioning is a powerful tool that we use to engage students in a task, to encourage students to extend their thinking, to evaluate our instruction, and to gauge student learning. However, some students become uncomfortable when confronted with a question. Many students assume that if a teacher questions their thinking, there must be an error. This is largely due to past experiences. Some students are accustomed to only being questioned when their work is incorrect. They perceive questions as an interruption in the flow of the class period. How many times have you said to a student, "Are you sure?" and they immediately lose confidence in their work? It's important to change this perception. Students need to learn not only to respond to teachers' questions but also to pose questions of one another and of themselves. As adult learners, we often pose questions to others and ourselves as we work through a problem. Such inquiries serve as a means to build, clarify, and extend our understanding. A good rule of thumb is to follow all student answers with a question, whether

Can Collections

**Maria and Stephen collected cans for a recycling
project in their neighborhood. Maria collected 24
cans, while Stephen collected 8 cans. How many
times more cans did Maria collect than Stephen?
Draw a picture to show your solution.**

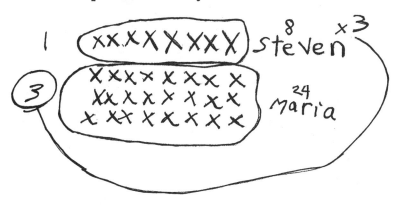

Figure 2–11 *Ellen applied a multiplication strategy by connecting ideas of arrays,
basic facts, and division.*

right or wrong. Questioning is a skill to be developed. Share with students some
of the questions you ask of others and of yourself. Help them to understand that
it should be a lifelong practice. Help them realize that "to question is to learn."

Questions for Discussion

1. What prerequisite skills/ideas are necessary for student success with the math
    concepts you are currently teaching?

2. How is your planning process affected by the interconnected nature of math-
    ematics?

3. What criteria should you consider when choosing the materials and manip-
    ulatives made available to students during instruction?

4. How can you remind yourself to ask more and tell less?

5. How will acquisition of the concept or skill you are about to introduce help
    students acquire a more complex level of knowledge for later grades?

CHAPTER 3

Mathematics Connections
to Other Disciplines

The development of mathematical ideas and the use of mathematics in other disciplines are intertwined.

—National Council of Teachers of Mathematics,
Principles and Standards for School Mathematics

Foundation Skills and Varied Components of This Standard

During the teaching of language arts, science, social studies, and even art, music, and physical education, mathematics concepts and skills can be introduced, reinforced, and revisited. While it may take a bit of planning for you to do this, the impact on student understanding and the sense-making that comes as a result, are well worth the time. Teachers say that in doing this they can actually spend more time reinforcing many important mathematics skills.

Language Arts and Mathematics

Language arts skills (speaking, reading, listening, and writing) are easily integrated into mathematics instruction. The more often we ask students to justify their answers and listen to one another share problem-solving strategies, the closer we are to integrating these two areas of the curriculum. And, having students represent what they have just done through illustrations and words gives them a chance to write to explain or write to describe. Mathematics and language arts haven't always been closely aligned. With the NCTM *Principles and Standards for School Mathematics* (NCTM 2000) teachers have been encouraged to create lessons in which all of these language arts skills are practiced. Griffiths and Clyne (1991, 3) agree: "Children learn mathematics through using language, therefore opportunities for discussion during all stages of mathematical learning are important." And, it isn't just discussion that contributes to the understanding that students take from mathematics lessons. Often by the time students enter third grade they are able to express themselves in writing in a way that primary students cannot. Writing "taps into" their understandings in that it forces them to reflect on what they know and what they believe about different mathematics ideas.

There are many benefits to connecting mathematics and language arts. Listening to a story is appealing to students of all ages and often provides them with a structure within which to explore mathematical ideas. And stories provide a rich context for later mathematics problems.

Knowing where to find resources for literature selections and ideas to incorporate writing into your lesson is one part, but what is it that you need to know to effectively make use of classroom time? And what concepts can be enriched by connecting them to literature and writing?

It's almost common sense that you'd need to have a good understanding of the mathematics curriculum that you're teaching (across the standards). If you do then it's easy to see how learning about the solar system in science would lend itself to reinforcing subtraction as students determine the difference between the distance of the Earth to the Sun and Mercury, Venus, and Pluto's distance to the Sun. And, why not do this? Students are fascinated by big numbers and since they are learning about the solar system anyway it makes sense to give them some computational practice while they are finding out about the planets. And, if you're familiar with all of the science content that you are expected to teach during the year, you can find ways to reinforce computation even before you get to your mathematics unit on computation.

Knowing the yearlong mathematics curriculum isn't enough though. If you're to be successful connecting mathematics across the curriculum, you need to know the curriculum from each discipline being taught. What are all of the social studies units of study that students will be learning about, and where is there a direct link to mathematics? Are there indirect links that can be made? This research takes planning and careful reflection, but most teachers remark how easy it really was to do and how much mathematics was reinforced. Mathematics can actually be imbedded in the social studies unit, which means it doesn't need to be "taught" again during mathematics time. You can remind yourself, when you get to that unit in your curriculum and/or textbook, that you've already taught this concept or skill and that it need not be taught again. You may want to make certain that your students still remember, or have truly learned this skill, during their social studies unit. But, it's likely that they will have, and you now have more time to focus on skills and concepts that need to be introduced.

Mathematics inherent in each curricular area demonstrates to us all how easy it is to find ways to teach the mathematics we are expected to teach. You can find examples of this inherent math in such things as patterns in poetry; measurement and data collection in science; mapping skills in geography; meter, pitch, and rhythm in music; shape, proportion, and pattern in art; and timing and measurement in physical education.

So, we need to learn how to

- identify all of the mathematics inherent in other curricular areas

- integrate them in such a way that both subjects are supported soundly

- document the learning and assess these understandings

Let's look at each curricular area and see how some teachers are making these connections. Additional ideas and activities will be found on the CD, with suggestions of websites and resource materials that can further support this way of teaching.

Connection with Language Arts

Many mathematical ideas take shape through our attempts at communicating about them (orally and in writing). No longer do students and teachers resist the idea of writing during mathematics class. And, "with such a clear emphasis on understanding and communicating, it shouldn't be surprising that math teachers have been turning to writing" (Countryman 1992, 10). It makes sense to be mindful of the language arts inherent in a lesson.

And, while students of any age enjoy being read to, this doesn't take place in the intermediate grades as often as it does in primary grades. Time constraints prevent many teachers from deviating from their established curriculum or for setting aside time to read aloud to their students. Getting everything "done" by the time students are tested has many teachers racing through content without looking for enriching experiences. Yet, when a piece of math-related literature is used, to springboard into a lesson, students have a context in which to make sense out of problems posed. And since sense-making is imperative for students to be able to apply the skills and concepts they are learning about, a piece of literature may be a key element in making this happen.

Often when lessons have a reading component, all areas of language arts are imbedded in the lesson. While younger students may have some difficulty writing about what they've done, or what they know, in the intermediate grades students should be expected to put their strategies and mathematical thoughts on paper.

Writing is "thinking made visible"—so students' written explanations and strategies can provide teachers with glimpses into what students know and do not know about the mathematics concepts and skills being introduced. This serves as a powerful assessment device as it gives teachers greater clarity when making instructional decisions. And having students take the time to reflect on what it is they have done to solve a problem, or write about the strategy they have used to get an answer, helps students create more meaning for themselves. Not to mention that every student gets to participate when everyone is writing during mathematics. Students can't sit back and let others respond when all students are involved.

Activity: Connecting Literature, Writing, and Geometry/Number Sense

Students in third through fifth grade have been introduced to both plane and solid geometric figures during their experiences in the primary grades. Often they have tested solid shapes to see if they can stack, spin, slide, and roll, and they have identified them within their environments. If students have not had opportunities to explore with many of these figures they may have a limited understanding of what makes a polygon a polygon and a polyhedron a polyhedron. It's not unusual for a third grader to believe that "a hexagon is the yellow pattern block" and that other six-sided polygons "aren't really hexagons." It is also quite common to find students who believe that all rectangles have to have "two long sides and two short sides" and that squares, when rotated 45 degrees, are called "diamonds." These misconceptions may be due to the fact that students have had little exposure to shapes and their properties. In an article from *Teaching Children Mathematics*, Oberdorf and Taylor-Cox write about the misconceptions that students have, about geometry, and that these are frequently the result of what teachers have used as models. "These constructions may cause confusion later as educators clarify for children that squares also fit the description of rectangles" (Oberdorf and Taylor-Cox 1999, 340).

The book, *The Greedy Triangle* by Marilyn Burns, is an excellent resource to use to springboard into a lesson on plane figures. Using a geoboard and geobands, students can create the shapes that are being introduced in the story. Through this read-aloud, students see the effect of adding an additional side to each polygon that is made. If students do the same thing that the "greedy triangle" is doing (as the story is being read), multiple representations of shapes can be shared. Students will learn the names of the polygons and their attributes, but they will also learn that regular and irregular shapes share a name.

Let's look at the next activity to see how third-grade students represented various shapes as they listened to *The Greedy Triangle*. And, let's see if their writings reflect a clearer understanding of what makes a quadrilateral a quadrilateral and a triangle a triangle.

Each student is given a geoboard and one large geoband. After exploring with the band for several minutes, Ms. Taylor (a pseudonym) asks students to put their geoboards in "listening position" (with the pegs facing down on their desks) and the following discussion occurs.

TEACHER: What types of things were you able to do with your geoboard and geoband?
STUDENT: I made a design.
STUDENT: I made different shapes.
STUDENT: I made a star.
STUDENT: I stretched mine and made the biggest square that I could make.

Teachers tell us that they don't like using geoboards because students "fling the rubber bands around the room and snap them on each other." The following suggestions may help this behavior happen less often in your classroom. Prior to using a geoboard (even if students have used it in years past), ask students to think of things they can tell you about it. Then have them share how they've used them in the past, or what they think they could be used for—if they haven't ever used them before. Then show students a large colored geoband, call it a geoband, and let students know that there are appropriate and inappropriate ways to use this band. Tell them that these bands can snap (on friends or on them) if they aren't careful to keep one finger on one part of it at all times (until the band is securely on the pegs). Demonstrate how this is done and put the geoboard down. Next show students a piece of geoboard paper (see Geoboard Paper in the Additional Tools section on the CD) and let them know that this paper will be given to anyone who cannot use the geoboard and geoband in a safe and appropriate manner. This is a proactive way to deal with the possibility that the band or board may be used in a less than mathematical way.

It's clear that students enjoyed being able to explore with this manipulative before they would use it as a "learning tool." Ms. Taylor then says, "I've got this wonderful book to share with you today. Let's go to the floor to hear this story." The students sit on the rug, to listen to the story without the distraction of the geoboard.

"The title of this book is *The Greedy Triangle*. Think for a few seconds about what the word *greedy* means," Ms. Taylor asks her students. Ten seconds are given to think about this term and then students discuss with the person next to them their thoughts about this word. Ms. Taylor asks students if they would like to share what they had been thinking about, or share something that they had heard from their partner. The students had the following to say.

STUDENT: Me and Tanishia were talking about *greedy* means always wanting more of something—like you get some cookies and then you act "all greedy" and want more.

STUDENT: We thought that *greedy* was like grabbing stuff.

STUDENT: No, *greedy* is being selfish and never liking what you already have.

Ms. Taylor then says that she will be reading the story and students can find out if their ideas about what *greedy* means make sense. She tells them that the first time the story is read they will just listen and look at the pages. She asks them to listen for the names of the different shapes that the triangle asks the "shape shifter" to turn him into. She tells them that she will read the story a second time and they'll be able to use their geoboards to create the shapes that they hear about in the story. As you read, you will sometimes hear them whispering to each other the names of the shape that will be made next. Many students know that a five-sided polygon is called a pentagon, and that a six-sided polygon is called a hexagon. But, no one knows that a seven-sided polygon is called a heptagon and there's a "buzz" as Ms. Taylor says the word.

STUDENT: I thought it'd be called a *septagon*.
TEACHER: Tell everyone what made you think that this would be the shape's name.
STUDENT: I don't know, maybe because *seven* starts with an *s*, and I thought that a seven-sided figure would also start with an *s*.
TEACHER: Isn't it interesting how we connect certain things to what we already know?

Once the story has been read, from beginning to end, Ms. Taylor asks students to recall what happened during the story, and if they think they now know what *greedy* means. "It's like what Jamarcus and Tanishia were saying; you always want what you don't have. The triangle was kind of spoiled. It was never really happy with what it was." The discussion continues with Ms. Taylor asking questions about the names of all of the shapes that the triangle became. As these names are given, she writes them on chart paper (leaving room for some illustrations that will provide students with something visual to remember the shape).

Students return excitedly to their seats and turn their geoboards to "working position" (with the pegs facing up), ready to listen to the story, again, and make the different shapes with the geoband. As the story is reread, Ms. Taylor has different students hold up their geoboards so all students can see the different types of quadrilaterals, pentagons, hexagons, and so on, that are being made.

Ms. Taylor's questions help students construct a clearer understanding of the attributes necessary for a shape to have a specific name. She asks, "So does it matter that Rodrigo's hexagon doesn't look like the one from the pattern blocks that we use?"

Figure 3–1 *Devon proudly shows his pentagon.*

"It still has six sides," says Rodrigo, "so it's still called a hexagon."

Ms. Taylor reinforces this by asking, "So, all closed figures with six straight sides will be called hexagons?" While some students appear surprised, most are using the "me too" sign language sign, indicating that they agree.

The lesson continues with students making each of the shapes until they cannot make any more. They wait as the teacher reads the ending of the story, relieved that they can make a triangle again—a shape that is easy to make on a geoboard. Geoboard paper is given to each student and the lines on the bottom provide students with a place to write their ideas. (Refer back to Geoboard Paper with Reflection in the Mathematical Ideas Interconnect and Build Upon One Another section on the CD.) Their assignment is to use their geoboard and create any type of triangle they wish to create. They are then to draw this same triangle onto the geoboard paper and explain how they know that this is a triangle. When they are finished writing about the triangle, they may explore with their geoband and geoboard or write something on the back of their paper explaining what the triangle in the story learned.

Jordyn's writing (Figure 3–2) shows her teacher that she understands what makes a triangle a triangle. It also shows her teacher that it doesn't matter what size or position the triangle is in, as long as it has three sides and three vertices.

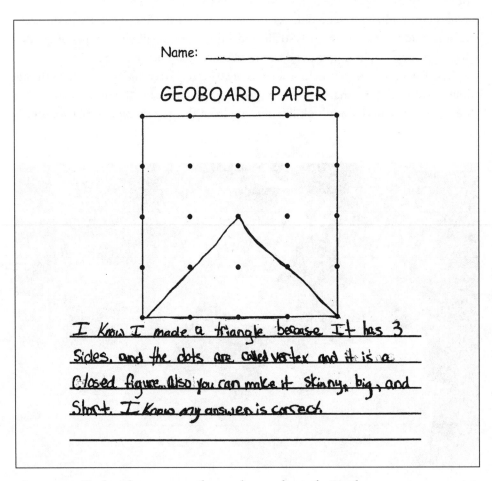

Figure 3–2 *Jordyn demonstrates her understanding of triangles.*

Ronald's explanation includes the word *edges*, which lets Ms. Taylor know that he is confused about what to call the sides of a plane figure. But, as the students work, Ms. Taylor is impressed with how attentive they are and how engaged they are in this work. It is clear to her that her students have enjoyed and learned from this activity.

By connecting literature and writing to the mathematics lesson, Ms. Taylor is able to develop a context for clarifying the attributes needed for a triangle to be called a triangle, and she is able to provide students with the opportunity to create different polygons and compare what they've made with what a friend has made. Student's written explanations show Ms. Taylor that she can move on in their study of shapes since it's clear that her students understand the definitions of these terms. And, by reading the back of some of their assignments, she can also see that they learned another lesson as well. Dorrian wrote the following on the back of his paper, "The triangle in the book learned to be satisfied about his shape and to be who he is." Wouldn't it be wonderful if all students accepted themselves for who they are? Marilyn Burns says, "Incorporating children's books into mathematics instruction helps students experience the wonder possible in mathematical problem solving and helps them see a connection between mathematics and the imaginative ideas in books" (1992, 1).

Figure 3–3 *Bianca explains how she made a triangle.*

Manipulatives play such an important role in helping students represent what they know and understand. Even when they aren't being misused, it's difficult for students to listen to someone explaining what they've made on their geoboard given the temptation to continue to work on what they are creating. We've found that the best way to avoid these problems is to set up rules before even handing geoboards out to students. Included in the rules is knowing about the difference between "working position" and "listening position." "Working position" involves having the geoboard with the pegs facing up—making it possible to use a geoband and create shapes on the board. "Listening position" involves turning the geoboard upside down so that the pegs are either on the desk, in the student's lap, or on the floor. This prevents students from continuing to create shapes with their bands, and encourages active listening.

Some math-related literature selections can be used to provide number sense and problem-solving practice for students who are used to computing in a traditional manner, and/or counting objects one at a time. In many of Greg Tang's books, pictures and text provide clues to students on how to think differently about numbers. In *The Grapes of Math,* his pages provide an engaging introduction to any mathematics lesson. With each colorful illustration, students are asked to figure out how many, without counting by ones. Here's an example:

> *Fish School*
>
> Of all the creatures in the sea,
> A fish is smart as smart can be.
>
> While others swim and play it cool,
> A fish is happy in a school!
>
> How many fish are in this class?
> Answer quick and you will pass.
>
> Here's a hint, a little clue,
> When counting fish, just look askew!

While Greg Tang does provide "an answer" at the end of the book, it is students' responses to this question and the strategies that they use to get their answer that are so amazing to hear. Mr. Tang's strategy for figuring out how many fish there are is to look at the four diagonals of four fish and know that four groups of four equal sixteen.

"That's a cool strategy," said Raymond when he heard that this was what the author and illustrator were thinking as the book was written. "But, I did it a different

Figure 3–4 *Illustration accompanying the poem "Fish School"*

way," he said, with great confidence. "Here's what I did. See, I saw there were doubles, with a four in the middle."

"How did that help you get the answer of sixteen?" I asked.

"OK, see one doubled that's two. Two doubled, that's four. So far that's six—easy. Then three doubled that's another six. Now I've got six plus six and that's twelve—another double. Add four more and you've got your sixteen." It's these sorts of strategies that the pictures in Greg Tang's books promote.

Using a good piece of children's literature (whether it's one written specifically to reinforce mathematics concepts and skills or one that's just used to springboard into a mathematics lesson) provides a teacher with so many exciting ways to practice both mathematics and language arts skills.

Social Studies and Mathematics

In some of the schools we've visited, social studies is nearly eliminated as a subject students study. This is one of those facts we find very hard to understand. When we were in school we learned about Native Americans, Greek civilization, Maryland (our state), and U.S. history. I can still recite the preamble of the Constitution. How can it be that some students today are never exposed to these same things?

53

Well, many state assessments only test language arts and mathematics skills. If the subjects aren't going to be tested, some believe, time shouldn't be spent teaching them. This is such a shame given how much students learn by studying the history of their own state and the United States, the inventors who paved the way for things we rely on daily, and how people live in other countries and cultures. So, if your school does not include social studies in its curriculum the opportunity to teach students many social studies concepts can be done through mathematics connections.

The NCTM encourages finding examples of mathematics in other cultures as well as finding ways to connect social studies ideas into the mathematics curriculum (NCTM 2000, 201). The NCTM wrote, "Since our schools have increasingly heterogeneous populations from many different cultures around the world, an apparently European-based curriculum can be counterproductive to our interest in recruiting members of underrepresented groups into mathematics" (1995, 34).

So, whether it's to increase student awareness about mathematics in other societies or to provide a real-life context for problem-solving activities, making a connection with social studies has real benefits for students.

Activity: Solidifying Place Value Understanding by Learning Other Numeration Systems

We thought that by the time students entered fourth grade that they would have a fairly clear understanding of the base ten place value system and that they would appreciate how useful it is in representing numbers. What we found instead was that students had memorized the "periods" that exist and given no thought whatsoever about our simple to understand system of numeration. Sure students could identify the one's place, hundred's place, and even read and write numerals in the millions. But, did they "get" that our system of numeration has only ten digits and that those digits and the places they occupy allow us to write any numeral? It seemed like they didn't. So, we decided to create a unit of study in which students would learn different numeration systems and then compare these with the base ten system. Our hope was that this would help them better understand our place value system making sense-making easier in a later study of decimal numbers.

Our unit began by looking at Egyptian Numerals. (See Egyptian Numeration System in the Mathematics Connections to Other Disciplines section on the CD). This additive system of numeration is fairly simple to learn. The symbols are easy to draw, and the fact that it takes forever to write 999 brought "home" to our students that this was not a very efficient system. It was not uncommon to hear moans whenever they saw a Hindu-Arabic Numeral that had the digit six or higher. Students knew that they would be drawing a lot of some symbol, or counting to figure out the Hindu-Arabic counterpart.

The following chart helped us keep track of the different systems we were learning about:

Name of System	Type of System	Number of Symbols Used	Symbols Used	Pros and Cons
Egyptian Numeration System	Additive	Symbols for 1, 10, 100, 1000, 10,000, 100,000, 1,000,000	(Egyptian hieroglyph symbols)	Symbols were fun to draw Too many symbols were needed for digits greater than 5 and you ended up having to count them to know what the number was
Roman Numeral System	Partially additive (when the numeral 4 or 9 appeared it was subtractive)	Symbols for 1, 5, 10, 50, 100, 500, 1,000 then a line segment above a numeral meant to multiply by 1,000.	I, V, X, L, C, D, M	Not that many symbols to learn Forget to subtract when 4 and 9 were in a numeral
Japanese Numeration System	Multiplicative	Symbols for 1, 2, 3, 4, 5, 6, 7, 8, 9, 10, 100, 1000 . . .	一 二 三 四 五 六 七 八 九 十 百 千	Symbols were like art; such fun to draw Easy to read the numeral Hard to remember what the symbols meant
Mayan Numerals	Additive and multiplicative	Only three used; symbols for 1, 5, 20	A dot, a dash, and an oval	Easy to remember the symbols Hard to remember how to use the symbols

Then we reviewed some of the Roman numerals that many had learned in third grade (or at least they'd been exposed to them). Students practiced writing Roman numerals, given Hindu-Arabic numerals and writing Hindu-Arabic numerals given their Roman counterparts. As expected fours and nines (regardless of the place either was in), gave them trouble and when asked to write 494, many wrote: CCCCLXXXXIIII. But, they loved learning that a line segment above a symbol meant that the symbol was now one thousand times its size. And, suddenly the sound of, "Give us a harder one!" was being spoken by lots of students. Decoding Roman numerals, to figure out what the Hindu-Arabic numeral was seemed to be more of a puzzle than a problem and students were motivated to work together to figure these out.

"What does it mean if you have two line segments over a symbol?" Sharnita asked me, during the second day of this study.

"What do you think it means?" I asked the class. "Talk with the people at your table and see if you can figure out what it might mean if two line segments are above a symbol. Remember that one means that you multiply the numeral times one thousand."

"We need calculators for this," several students said. And, they got these out of the cabinet so they could do their figuring.

Did students figure out what these would mean? Of course. And, in the course of studying about Roman numerals we learned a lot about counting by different quantities, multiplying by one thousand, and even some facts about Roman civilization. Thanks to almanacs and websites, information is readily available to anyone who knows how to surf the Web. The following websites are useful for finding activities and ideas:

http://mathforum.org/paths/measurement/cold.html (lessons on graphing and weather)

www.lessonplanspage.com/SS45.htm (fifteen pages into the site there is a section labeled "Math Connections")

http://sin.fi.edu/time/keepers/Silverman/html/RomanMatch.html (online activities using Roman numerals)

http://score.kings.k12.ca.us/lessons/ponyexp.him (activities using the Pony Express)

http://worldatlas.com/webimage/countrys/nariv.htm (provides information about lengths of rivers from around the world)

We could have spent a full week looking at calligraphy and the making of Japanese numerals, not to mention that this could have given us an entry into studying Japanese civilization. Students were captivated by how beautiful each symbol was and loved using a paint brush and black tempura paint to do mathematics. And, knowing that a number such as 432 was made by first representing the symbol for four, and then the symbol for one hundred made a lot of sense to students who were finally seeing the difference between the "face" of a numeral and its "place." But, time was a factor, and the focus of our study was not on these ancient civilizations, but rather on comparing different numeration systems to the one that we use daily.

Finally, we looked at Mayan numerals. Students found that the simplicity of the system made it a more difficult one to understand. But, they practiced it enough to be able to see how it was used to create different multidigit numerals.

At the end of this study (and it lasted for about seven days) what did students learn?

"We have the best system for writing numbers," Bryan said.

"What makes you think that?" I asked.

"Cause I know it and it wasn't that hard to learn," he grinned broadly.

"OK," I said, "But, who else thinks that the Hindu-Arabic system is the best and you've got a different reason for saying this?"

"It's not just cause we know it, it's because it's easy. You only need to know 0, 1, 2, 3, 4, 5, 6, 7, 8, and 9. Those are pretty easy to draw. And, those are the only numbers that get used over and over making as many numbers as you can make."

"You don't need to remember rules for different numbers, like with Roman numerals," Sara said.

In this unit of study mathematics was the focus, but social studies and other civilizations were also introduced. In the intermediate grades, how else can social studies be incorporated into mathematics class? Timelines can be used to represent the passage of time, giving historical dates more meaning. How many years ago did Robert Fulton build the first successful steamship, if he did this in 1807? In 1903 Orville and Wilbur Wright's "Flyer" flew for just under a minute. Was this more or less than a century from the time that astronauts landed on the moon? The Volkswagen "Beetle" began being mass produced in 1937 in Germany. When did this car arrive in the United States? What is the average number of "Beetles" sold in a year?

Do students know that the U.S. postal system began around 1840? Postage stamps and regular mail deliveries were introduced at this time. Have students figure out how many years ago this was and research the route that a letter takes from the time it is sent to the time that it arrives at someone's home. Comparing international and national postage stamps gives students some idea of the types of things popular in the country where the stamp originated. In James Burnett and Calvin Iron's *Mathematics on the Move* (1997, 11) the following chart gives students a sense of the number of post offices found in different countries:

Country	Post Offices
Australia	4,400
Canada	18,500
India	150,000
New Zealand	950
United Kingdom	19,600
USA	38,000

Having students speculate about why India has so many post offices would make an excellent writing project. Figuring out how many miles a light aircraft flies in a year, given its 1,615 mile trip across the Australian outback each week, would also raise some interesting questions. Facts like these fascinate students and make mathematics come alive—in a way that textbook problems cannot.

Mathematics also helps students visualize the relative magnitude and comparative size of landforms, bodies of water, states, countries, and continents. Students who understand coordinate geometry are better equipped to understand longitude, latitude, and other mapping concepts. As students begin learning about using degrees to measure a circle, why not have them look at who developed this system and how it came about. More than 2,300 years ago the Babylonians devised this system for dividing up a circle. Did they choose 360 degrees because their year had 360 days, or was it because their numeration system involved grouping in sixties?

Economics cannot be taught without an understanding of trends, statistics, knowledge of money, and skill with operating on numbers. And, Colonial hex signs, quilting, and other crafts use knowledge of patterning, geometry, and measurement. The connection with social studies provides teachers with powerful real-world uses of mathematics.

Science and Mathematics

Can you even imagine studying science without using mathematics? Mathematics is needed to determine the distance between the planets and the sun, the patterns and forecasts associated with weather, or the growth of plants given different variables (sunlight, or lack thereof, water, or lack thereof). Physics, chemistry, biology, and environmental science are all dependent on some knowledge of every content standard in the *Principles and Standards for School Mathematics*. Students often don't see these connections and sometimes we fail to note these connections. Perhaps it is because these were never really pointed out to us. So, let's look at some science units that are often taught in the intermediate grades and note all of the ways that mathematics can be integrated. These connections will provide you with an answer to a question that students often ask—"When will I ever use this?"

Most science involves making predictions, gathering information (data) from various investigations, experimenting, and finally analyzing the collected data. To us that sounds like many of the mathematical investigations that we've created or observed. And, just as you wouldn't use a protractor to measure the height of a structure, science experiments require that students know which tools to use to carry out specific experiments as well. It would be silly to check the temperature of a liquid with a magnifying glass and just as silly to use a ruler to measure the mass of certain rocks.

Other similarities that exist between mathematics and science are in students' needing to know whether their results seem reasonable and how to communicate and describe what they've done to complete an experiment. They need to know how to represent their conclusion. Models, diagrams, and charts, as well as symbols, are all used to display the results of a scientific experiment, just as they are used to detail the solution of a mathematics problem.

So, what types of math/science connections can be made at these grades? Let's look at the different areas of study and see how pointing out the mathematics would let students know the value of being able to think mathematically. In Earth and space science, students are exposed to the impact that weathering has on changing the surface of the Earth. They learn about earthquakes and volcanoes and their effects on the land, as well as humans' effect. And, they learn about the formation of mountains, rivers, canyons, and valleys and how to classify fossils.

To connect these areas to mathematics is not a "stretch." Students can use a timeline to show when various earthquakes occurred and volcanoes erupted. They can look at the destruction of each and the number of people who died. They can look at the height of a volcano prior to its eruption and its height afterward and they can certainly look to see if there are patterns to these occurrences. Students can use the following chart to see the highest mountains on each of the seven continents and determine the difference in height in feet. And, what a surprise students would have to find out that the world's tallest mountain is not one of the seven listed here but rather Mauna Kea, found in Hawaii. This mountain is 33,480 feet, but 19,684 feet is hidden below sea level (Burnett and Irons 1997, 7).

Continent	Mountain	Height in Feet
North America	Mount McKinley	20,320
South America	Mount Aconcagua	22,834
Africa	Mount Kilimanjaro	19,340
Europe	Mont Blanc	15,770
Asia	Mount Everest	29,022
Australia	Mount Kosciusko	7,314
Antarctica	Vinson Massif	16,066

Activity: Classifying Rocks and Minerals

Students can sort rocks and minerals by their type (igneous, sedimentary, and metamorphic). They can test and chart the color, luster, hardness, and streak of these rocks and then classify them in different ways. And, fossils can also be classified by whether they are animal or plant, found on water or land.

In the study of astronomy, students can study the magnitude of numbers by looking at the distance of each planet from the sun and from the Earth. Studying the temperature and climate changes of each planet gives students a clearer understanding of why similar life-forms that exist on the Earth do not exist on other planets. And, by looking at the repeating patterns of celestial events (day/night, the four seasons, and the stages of the moon) students are given a practical application of repeating patterns. In addition, students can use the following chart (from Burnett and Irons 1997, 2) to look at the number of days that the nine planets take to orbit the sun, and speculate as to why this is.

Planet	Days to Orbit the Sun
Mercury	88
Venus	225
Earth	365
Mars	687
Jupiter	4,329

Planet	Days to Orbit the Sun
Saturn	10,753
Uranus	30,664
Neptune	60,158
Pluto	90,411

Can't you just imagine how much practice students would get with estimation and then division by looking at the number of orbits and comparing this with Earth? If the Earth were to only take 225 days to orbit the Sun (as Venus does), that would be about two-thirds of a year. If the Earth were to take 4,329 days (as Jupiter does) that would be a bit less than twelve years! Those kinds of statistics are fascinating for fifth graders, who don't mind dividing to figure out this information.

The idea of classifying, sorting, and charting is also done as students test the measurable properties of an element's ability to conduct heat, attract magnets, or have an electrical charge. And the statement, "No matter how many parts of an object are assembled, the mass of the whole object made is always the same as the sum of the parts," can easily be connected to mathematical ideas of equality. Using a bucket balance and metric weights it's simple to test the weight of a whole rock and then the same rock split into pieces. Ideas of equality can be connected to science as well as to mathematics.

Making predictions, devising an experiment, and then analyzing the outcomes of the experiment can be done as students study physical and chemical changes of a variety of things. When vinegar is combined with baking soda is it likely that a student would predict what would happen? Perhaps not, but when a different white power (talc) is combined with the same vinegar, might not the student predict that the same bubbling would occur? This testing of predictions, based on prior experiences, happens often in mathematics as it does in science.

Here's just one example of what we mean by this. In second grade, students begin to look for patterns and relationships that exist between the operations of addition and subtraction. After they've added many single-digit numbers they often conclude the following:

■ Adding an even number to another even number produces a sum that is even.

■ Adding an odd number to another odd number produces a sum that is even.

■ Adding an odd number to an even number produces a sum that is odd.

When they are in fourth grade, many students carry over this idea to multiplication of numbers. They predict that the same thing will happen with numbers, when they multiply as had happened when they added. It's the savvy teacher who says, "What would you like to do to test out your theory?" Then, of course, as students see what happens with single-digit factors they come to the conclusion that:

■ Multiplying an even number by another even number produces a product that is even.

- Multiplying an even number by an odd number produces a product that is even.
- Multiplying an odd number by an odd number produces a product that is odd.

Just as is done in science, a prediction is made (often based on background knowledge) and then some experiment is conducted to test out this prediction.

And, in the study of mechanics, students are often involved in measurement activities as they determine and then compare the distances that moving objects (traveling at different speeds) will travel. When variables such as texture of a surface or height of an inclined plane are added, students are likely to predict, test, and perhaps come up with a formula for determining the effect of these changes. Berlin and White write,

> Science seeks to advance knowledge through the observation and manipulation of phenomena in order to explore the nature of the environment and human existence in that environment. Science searches for consistent and verifiable patterns to build a knowledge base and explain the real world. (1995, 23–24)

When it's pointed out to them, students can see these same activities in mathematics experiments, and they can see mathematics being used within the science activities they are doing.

Art and Mathematics

Why should an art teacher, who may not be the classroom teacher, make sure that students know that they are doing mathematics when they are involved in certain art activities? Again, it relates to the idea that students often think that they are only doing mathematics during math class. They are unaware that artists draw the human body based on specific proportions (and that these proportions are mathematical). They are surprised when they find out that drawings can be enlarged or reduced by plotting points on a grid and creating a proportional rendition of an illustration. And, while they may be attracted to designs that are symmetric or balanced, they may not realize that this is because the artist or craftsperson has used mathematics in this creation. And, they also may not realize the number of things, in nature, that are symmetric.

What sorts of art/mathematics activities are appropriate for the intermediate student and how can mathematics be imbedded in these activities? *Tessellations* (an arrangement of polygonal regions covering a plane without overlapping or leaving gaps) can be made with pattern blocks or colored paper. Making these provides students with opportunities to rotate, translate, and reflect shapes, as well as determine that the degree measures, around the common point of the angles of the figures, total 360 degrees. These geometry and measurement concepts are more readily understood when students are actually moving the shapes around. And, creating tessellations allows them to do this. If the teacher brings in tessellations created by Escher students begin to see the real-life connection between art and mathematics.

Quilting, basket making, and tapestry work is often connected to social studies. But, these artifacts can definitely be connected to mathematics as well. Students can select the fabric needed to create the quilt, cut pieces into squares and triangles so that they fit together, measure borders for sewing (since this will be done "by hand") and then sew a specific number of stitches per inch so the quilt will hold together. The practical application of knowing about repeating patterns, translation of shapes, linear measure, area, and perimeter are all required when making a quilt.

Architecture, again often associated with social studies, can be appreciated more seriously when looking at the symmetry of buildings, the designs and patterns used in brick and stone work, the triangular supports that prevent the building from collapsing, and the placement of windows and doors allowing for paths to be followed when entering or exiting.

Coordinate geometry is learned, with enthusiasm, when students are allowed to select a photograph, magazine picture, or cartoon character and enlarge it by plotting points on a grid. (See Coordinate Cartoons in the Mathematics Connections to Other Disciplines section on the CD.)

Origami and paper folding give students a chance to create different end products from a whole that begins as a square. The notion of part–whole is reinforced as students take the square and either fold it or cut it apart. Not only are the names of shapes reinforced but students may also get practice with fractional parts of a whole region, and spatial problem solving.

Let's look, in detail, at a fifth-grade class involved in the making of a set of tangrams. *Tangrams* are "a Chinese mathematical puzzle. The pieces of the puzzle are called *tans*. The finished arrangements made from the pieces are called tangrams. Tangrams of animal shapes, rectangles, triangles, parallelograms, trapezoids, hexagons, quadrilaterals, pentagons, and other designs can be made using the seven tans" (Nichols and Schwartz 1999, 408). Fractional parts of the whole square were revisited (since they had been taught earlier in the year) and then a problem-solving activity was posed, once the full set of tangrams were made.

Activity: Problem Solving with Tangrams

I began the lesson by asking the students if they had ever used a set of tangrams before. Surprisingly no one said that they had. I described the plastic pieces that are commonly found in most schools but was met with questioning looks on the faces of these fifth graders. I realized that this was going to be a brand-new experience for them, rather than a chance to revisit something they had done in an earlier grade.

Each student was given a square of green paper that measured $8\frac{1}{2}$ inches on each side.

"What are some ways that this square can be folded in half?" I asked.

"Down the middle," Kyle said, using his finger to show a vertical fold.

"Or if you turned the square the other way it would be this way," Nyllia said, indicating a horizontal fold.

"What shape would the halves be if you folded the square horizontally or vertically?" I asked.

The word *rectangle* was said by nearly every student.

I then said, "I want you to fold your square in half so that the halves are two congruent triangles." Students looked at one another as they brought the vertices together to fold the square in half across the diagonal. With scissors they cut these two triangles apart and I then asked them to put them back together to make their square. Was I ever surprised to see that some had difficulty doing this! Using words like *turn and flip,* one of the students described what was done to make the square again. Then I asked them to use these same pieces to make a larger triangle that was *similar* to the halves that they had made. There were even more problems doing this. But, once someone at the table had figured it out, the others looked to see how the two triangles were put together and got theirs to do the same thing. Finally I asked them to make a parallelogram that was not a rectangle.

"I don't get it," De'Sean said out loud. Several others echoed that same thing. "So, what do I mean by a 'parallelogram that isn't a rectangle'?" I asked the students. "Talk with the people at your table and see if you can describe the kind of shape I'm asking you to make."

While students talked, others at their table were moving the two triangles around and parallelograms were created.

"What part of the whole square is one of the triangles that we cut?" I asked. All students agreed that each triangle was one-half of the whole square. I drew the whole square on the chalkboard and told them that as we made each of the seven tans (from the set of tangrams) we were going to determine what fractional part of the whole square each piece represented. At the time this seemed to make sense to the students. But, this was before the pieces were made.

"Let's take one of the triangles and fold it in half," I said. "We'll be making the two large triangles from the set of tangrams." No one had a problem doing this; the two large triangles were folded and cut apart. I then asked the students to put the three pieces back together to make their original square. Without help from their friends, students would have had a difficult time doing this. The question that followed gave me answers I never expected to get. "Take 10 seconds and think about the fraction that describes each of the two large triangles from the set of tangrams. What part of the whole square is one of the triangles?"

After they had their thinking time I had students find a partner at their table and I listened to amazing answers. (Right now you may be thinking about the misconceptions that students often have about fractions, and you'd be correct.) The answers that I heard were one-half, one-third, two-thirds, one-fourth, and "I don't know." With questioning about what it means to be a fractional part of a whole region, the group came to a consensus that each large triangle, from the set of tangrams, was one-quarter of the entire square. I labeled the two large triangles that had been drawn on the chalkboard and proceeded to tell them that from the other half of the square would come the other five tangram pieces.

With each fold and tear, students were asked to talk about what fractional part of the whole square was the piece. Students were also asked to name the shape that was left after the piece that was just made had been cut off. The words *trapezoid, square, isosceles right triangle,* and *parallelogram* were all reinforced as students made a set of tangrams. In addition, they got continued practice with spatial problem solving as they were asked to put the square back together again, after each piece was made.

When all seven pieces had been cut, and the fractions associated with them had been written (on the chalkboard set of tangrams), I told them that they were going to use this information to solve a problem.

Figure 3–5 *Students putting tangrams together*

Figure 3–6 *Students recording their answers to the tangram problem solving activity.*

Watching students work let me know that before they did this they were going to need to manipulate the pieces and create other shapes and figures. So, for ten minutes I had them manipulate their set of tangrams to see if they could make the same large triangle and parallelogram that they had made when they only had two large triangles. While they struggled somewhat, no one seemed particularly frustrated, and this was where the lesson needed to end. But, Ms. Lyons, their teacher, signaled that it was OK to continue and so against my better judgment I went on.

"Here's the problem that I now want you to work on," I said. "Suppose the entire square costs one dollar. Using what you know about the fractional parts that each piece represents, see if you can determine the cost of each piece." Students were given calculators and told to work with others at their table, recording their answers on a worksheet (see Problem Solving with Tangrams in the Mathematics Connections to Other Disciplines section on the CD).

Students stayed engaged, and they worked with one another. But few seemed to be using the information about the fractional parts of the square until questions were asked of them. De'Sean's lengthy response in Figure 3–7 demonstrates his ability to

---

Problem Solving with Tangrams Recording Sheet

We figured out these "costs" for each of the tangram pieces:

Each large triangle is: 25 ¢ each
The medium triangle is: 5 ¢
Each small triangle is: 15 ¢ each
The square is: 10 ¢
The parallelogram is: 5 ¢

This is how we figured out the cost of each piece:

We came up with our answer by first labeling each shape. We started with our two large triangles and found that they cost twenty five cents each. We then went on to the smaller triangles and found that they should cost 15¢ each. We found the medium triangle and parallelogram = 5¢ by themselfes, and lastly we found that the square equals 10¢.

Figure 3–7 *De'Sean's written explanation to the tangram problem*

(continues)

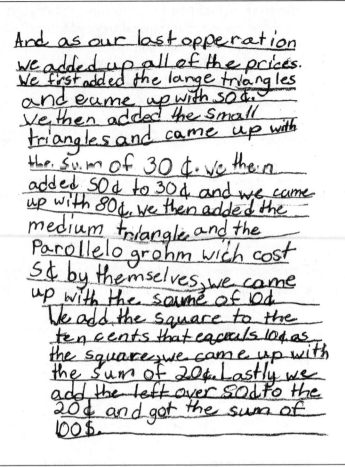

And as our last opperation we added up all of the prices. We first added the large triangles and came up with 50¢. We then added the small triangles and came up with the sum of 30¢. We then added 50¢ to 30¢ and we came up with 80¢. We then added the medium triangle and the Parollelo grohm wich cost 5¢ by themselves, we came up with the soume of 10¢. We add the square to the ten cents that eaceuls 10¢ as the square, we came up with the sum of 20¢. Lastly we add the left over 80¢ to the 20¢ and got the sum of 100$.

Figure 3–7 *Continued*

articulate what was done to arrive at a solution (and even how he checked to see that the total was a dollar). But, it also shows his need to use "nice" numbers for each piece's cost. Tasmine's written response gets him closer to the correct answers (see Figure 3–8). And Nillya and Shalonda show what they did to get correct answers to this problem (see Figure 3–9). (See also the Problem Solving with Tangrams Recording Sheet on the CD.)

The lesson took nearly two solid hours. And students got practice with

- spatial problem solving

- naming plane figures

- transformational geometry

- reviewing ideas of congruence and similarity

- fractional parts of a whole region

- decimals and money

- division

- area

And, while they revisited these mathematics concepts and skills, they were involved in an art-related activity using a popular mathematical puzzle.

Problem Solving with Tangrams Recording Sheet

We figured out these "costs" for each of the tangram pieces:

Each large triangle is:	25¢
The medium triangle is:	$12\frac{1}{2}$ ¢
Each small triangle is:	$6\frac{1}{4}$ ¢
The square is:	$12\frac{2}{4}$
The parallelogram is:	$18\frac{3}{4}$

This is how we figured out the cost of each piece:

• First we knew that a fraction is a part of a whole. Next when we saw the largest triangles we knew that they took up half the square. $1/2 = 50\%$, but since it was 2 triangle I divided by 2 and recieved a quotient of 25%. After that, I saw how much medium triangles can go into the large triangle. My quotient was 2, so I divide 25 by 2 and my quotient was 12 and $\frac{1}{2}$. Before I went to the square, I had to see how much small triangles could go into a medium triangle. This time my quotient was 6 and $\frac{1}{4}$. I knew 2 small triangles could go into a square, so I multiplied 6 and $\frac{1}{4}$ by 2 and my product was 12 and 2/4. Then I added all of the

Figure 3-8 *Tasmine's written response gets him closer to the correct answer.*

(continues)

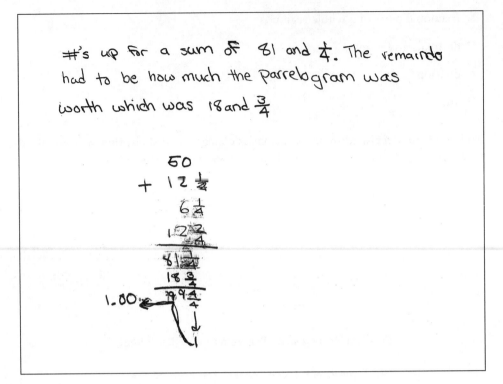

#'s up for a sum of 81 and ¼. The remainder had to be how much the parrelogram was worth which was 18 and ¾

Figure 3-8 *Continued*

Movement/Music and Mathematics

In the primary grades, students often get up and move around throughout their mathematics lessons (at least a lot more than students in the intermediate grades). But eight- through eleven-year-olds get fidgety too and need to be moving around (even if it's just to move from the rug to their seats and then back to the rug, at the end of a lesson).

There are a lot of mathematics concepts that lend themselves beautifully to movement-type lessons. Think about creating a walk-on grid that can be used to create real graphs, or can be used to get practice with coordinate geometry. And couldn't this same graph (if it was ten squares across and ten square down) be used as a hundreds chart to reinforce ideas about number relationships or decimal numbers? Arrow math, popular in the 1970s and 1980s, had students finding a numeral on a hundreds chart and then moving in the direction of the arrows to arrive on an ending numeral. With a walk-on hundreds chart students could walk in the direction of the arrows (or based on clues given by classmates or the teacher) to end on a specific numeral.

Here's what we mean. Have a student find the numeral 47 on the hundreds chart. Then say, "Find the number that is ten more. Then find the number that is one more than this. Finally, find the number that is two more than this. What number have you landed on?" The student will have moved below the 47 to the 57, then moved to the 58 and finally moved to the 60. This sort of activity done in third grade gives stu-

Problem Solving with Tangrams Recording Sheet

We figured out these "costs" for each of the tangram pieces:

Each large triangle is:	25¢
The medium triangle is:	12.5
Each small triangle is:	6¼
The square is:	12½
The parallelogram is:	12.5

This is how we figured out the cost of each piece:

We found our cost of each piece by looking our two large triangles it came up to 25¢. Then we looked at our medium triangle that came up to 12.5 by thinking what was half of 25 and 12.5 (12.5 + 12.5 = 25). We also knew that each small triangle equal 6¼ we knew this because half of 12 was 6 and half of ½ = ¼. Then we found out that our square equals to 12½. We knew it equaled to 12½ because I know that I measured the square to the other triangle and I got the answer 12½.

Figure 3–9 *Nillya and Shalonda explain how they got their correct answer.*

dents a clearer sense of where numbers are located and reinforces the relationship that exists between numbers.

A walk-on hundreds chart may be an impossibility if your classroom isn't particularly large. But a walk-on number line really does fit on the floor of most classrooms. And, this material is a wonderful way to introduce and reinforce the idea of rounding numbers to the nearest ten or hundred.

Activity: Rounding Numbers on a Walk-On Number Line

The number line can be made of masking tape. A zero and one hundred will be at opposite ends. Then students are each given index cards with numerals written on them.

The numerals are all of the "decade" numbers (10, 20, 30, 40, 50, 60, 70, 80, and 90), as well as numerals between zero and one hundred. Ask the person holding the 50 where he or she might place the card, and have the student explain how he or she knew to put it there. Then have the other "decade" students place their cards on the line. When all of these numerals are placed make sure that students like the way they are on the line and have someone adjust these if there seems to be larger spaces between any pair of numerals. Then ask the student holding the 31 to place their card where they believe it belongs. When this is done ask the student to explain how they know that this was the correct place to go. Then ask, "What are the two decade numerals that 31 is between?" When this question is answered ask, "Is 31 closer to the 30 or the 40?" When this question has been answered ask, "So, if we were to round the number 31 to the nearest ten (or decade number), which would it be rounded to?" It is likely that students will "see" this right away. But when all of the cards are placed on the line the idea of rounding to the nearest ten has been experienced by everyone. This same strategy can be used for rounding to the nearest hundred, or for placing fractions, decimals, or percents on a line and determining their order. The getting up and down and rearranging the cards helps student see more clearly the concept that is being introduced. And, when someone forgets how to round a number, a teacher's words of, "Remember when we used the walk-on number line to . . . " may jostle a faulty memory.

Movement can also be done by dancing repeating patterns, creating shapes with bodies, and sorting or classifying people into groups.

And, when can music be used to teach mathematics concepts? At The Summit School, in Edgewater, Maryland, students learn songs to recall the multiplication facts. It's not unusual to hear, "Three, six, nine, twelve, fifteen, eighteen, twenty-one, twenty-four, twenty-seven, and finally thirty," to the tune of the popular holiday song, "Silver Bells" as students compute. Silly you say. Maybe, but these students can recall their facts, and it's the melody of the music that makes this possible.

A music teacher can certainly reinforce patterns and fractions by reminding students that each note is read as part of a whole note and songs may have stanzas that repeat or grow. The system of musical notation was developed in 1026 by Guido d'Arezzo. This system indicates the length of notes and how the notes are organized to create specific rhythms.

Music teachers can also help students come up with their own theory about the sound that an instrument will make by using a xylophone, harp, and even a guitar and letting students hear that the longer the bar or string the lower the note. "Music is mathematics in motion," a friend of ours once said and the connection between these two areas of study is quite real.

"We do math all day long!" could be the statement that students make when mathematics is connected to other subjects throughout the day. And, why not have them saying this? There are real, valid ways to point out the mathematics in each area of the curriculum. And, the more this is done the more likely it will be that students see the usefulness of the mathematics they are learning—during mathematics class.

Questions for Discussion

1. How are you currently using literature and writing during your mathematics classes?

2. In what ways do your state's standardized tests require that students write to explain their responses following the solution of a mathematics problem?

3. Which social studies and science units lend themselves to making a connection to mathematics and what activities could you do?

Mathematics Connections
in Everyday Experiences

The importance of making mathematics more meaningful to students was recognized in Curriculum and Evaluation Standards for School Mathematics, *which calls for "opportunities to make connections so that students can use mathematics in their daily lives."*

—National Council of Teachers of Mathematics,
Assessment Standards for School Mathematics

Foundation Skills and Varied Components of This Standard

While students may not recognize that they use mathematics throughout their day, they can be made aware of the mathematics that they do by the activities that a teacher exposes them to. In a chapter of the 1995 NCTM Yearbook, *Connecting Mathematics Across the Curriculum*, Vincent P. Schielack, Jr. explores the impact of using hobbies to demonstrate, to students, the mathematics that gets used in their daily lives.

> Scale-model builders use the concepts of measurement, proportion, and similarity. Cross-stitch and needlework of all types use these same ideas, as well as the geometry of pattern reading and translation of a gridline, pattern to cloth. Musicians use the fractions involved in musical intervals and key signatures. Computer enthusiasts require the logic of programming and the knowledge of algorithms and estimation procedures. (NCTM 1995, 210)

In this chapter, Mr. Schielack uses card collecting to introduce and then reinforce ideas of probability. And, while many hobbies do use mathematical concepts so do everyday, real-life experiences. The following story comes to you from an independent school in Edgewater, Maryland. All of the students at this school are learning differently. They attend this school primarily because the teachers can offer them an opportunity to learn that cannot be offered to them in a public school setting. Class size is small (sometimes as few as two students in a mathematics class), and individual attention is given so that every student is able to learn. This remarkable school provides students with opportunities to make sense out of the mathematics that is being introduced, practiced, and reinforced.

Activity: A Garden to Remember Elizabeth

It's early spring in Ms. Peck's fifth-grade mathematics class and it's time to talk about how to raise money to plant Elizabeth's garden. Elizabeth is a former student who died of cancer two years before. Maintaining a living memorial was very important to her classmates and so a garden was created. It is now these fifth graders' responsibility to come up with a plan for raising money, purchasing seeds, planting the garden, and then maintaining it.

In preparing for this project, the class realized that they needed to generate a letter to the director of the school, Dr. Mele-McCarthy, to get her permission to host a fundraiser. The class decided that it wanted to have a bake sale (a popular thing to do at this school). But because of dietary restrictions that many students have, the class knew that it had to have whatever was prepared be healthy. And they had to get the approval of Dr. Mele-McCarthy. The following letter was written by the students:

April 25, 200X

Dear Dr. Mele-McCarthy,

We would like to enhance the garden of Elizabeth. We want to add flowers and fix the trail. We would like to have a fundraiser by selling muffins or a healthy snack. We would like to raise money for the garden. We want to do this because we want to show how special Elizabeth is. After we get the money we will need to buy flowers and mulch. We are doing this in Math class because we will need to use math to count the money, find the area and perimeter of the garden, and develop our budget.

The garden is important because when, like flowers, a wish is planted in the heart it always stays special. We would like to do this because we think this would be special for Elizabeth. Also, we think Elizabeth would appreciate our thinking about her and caring. We would honor her and make her special at Summit School. And, that is the type of school we are.

We would love for you to help us, too!

Thank you,

Ms. Peck's Math Class (Hayley, Maddy, Conor, Bashir, Bradley, Marcus, and Ms. Peck)

This letter was given to the school's director and Ms. Peck began a "hunt" for a muffin recipe (that's what the students decided they wanted to bake) that used very little sugar and no artificial ingredients. The perfect recipe was found online at epicurious.com and Ms. Peck told this to her students as she handed them the recipe for Healthy Blueberry and Banana Muffins (see the sheet of the same name in the Mathematics Connections in Everyday Experiences section on the CD).

Healthy Blueberry and Banana Muffins

Ingredients

(makes 12 muffins)
$1\frac{1}{2}$ cups all purpose flour
$\frac{1}{2}$ cup sugar
$\frac{1}{4}$ cup oat bran
2 teaspoons baking powder
$\frac{1}{2}$ teaspoon salt
1 cup mashed ripe bananas (about 3 bananas)
$\frac{1}{2}$ cup unflavored soy milk
1 large egg
2 tablespoons vegetable oil
2 teaspoons fresh lemon juice
$1\frac{1}{2}$ cups fresh blueberries or $1\frac{1}{2}$ cups frozen blueberries, unthawed (6 to 7 ounces)

Preparation

1. Preheat oven to 400°F.
2. Line 12 muffin cups with paper liners.
3. Combine flour, sugar, oat bran, baking powder, and salt in medium bowl; whisk to blend.
4. Place mashed bananas in large bowl.
5. Stir in soy milk, egg, oil, and lemon juice.
6. Mix in dry ingredients, then blueberries.
7. Divide batter among muffin papers.
8. Bake muffins until tester inserted into center comes out clean, about 20 minutes.
9. Turn muffins out onto rack and cool 10 minutes.
10. Serve warm or at room temperature.

Students read the recipe and decided that it sounded really yummy and seemed healthy since it didn't use a lot of sugar.

"Dr. Mele-McCarthy will probably approve this if we show it to her," Ms. Peck told her students. And, the students agreed that the director would probably let them bake these for the sale.

"So, should we just make twelve muffins?" Ms. Peck asked the class.

"No, we need a lot more if we are going to collect enough money to buy the seeds, plants, and mulch for Elizabeth's garden," Maddy said.

"Well, talk with your partner and see if you can figure out how many muffins we should probably make. And, be ready to defend your idea with a good reason."

The students seriously discussed how many muffins they thought they needed to make, but were stymied when they realized that they didn't know how many students and teachers were in the school. Ms. Peck stopped their conversations when she realized this. "It sounds like some of you are asking the same question about how many people might be buying these muffins. Do you know about how many people are at Summit School?" Students acknowledged that they really did not know and Ms. Peck told them that there are about one hundred students and about twenty-five adults. "So if each person buys only one muffin we'd need a 125 muffins," Bashir said.

"Yeah, but some people might not buy any muffins and some might want to buy more than one," Conor argued.

"So, how do you want to figure this out?" Ms. Peck asked the students. They reach for their calculators and begin punching in numbers. Students divided 125 by 12 and came up with mixed numerals.

"Is there a multiple of twelve, that's close to 125?" asked Ms. Peck. And, hands shot up in the air.

"We could just think of the number of people as 120!" Marcus said excitedly. "One hundred twenty would be ten times the recipe. We could just multiply this recipe by ten and make 120 muffins."

With this idea in mind pairs of students worked to take the original recipe and figure out what ten times the ingredients would be.

In addition to the work that was done to multiply the ingredients, students (for homework) were asked to estimate the price of the ingredients that would be needed. Then, in class, they went online to find out the actual cost of each of the ingredients. They also decided to increase their recipe so that they'd be making 144 muffins.

Then began the discussion of what their budget would be for the ingredients and what they'd charge for each muffin so they'd make enough money to buy the plants, mulch, and other supplies to fix up Elizabeth's garden. Bashir's written work summarizes what the children decided to do (see Figure 4–1).

Ms. Peck stated, "We will be making 144 muffins. It will cost us approximately $50.00 to make them. We will need about $50.00 to do our project. How much will we need to charge for the muffins?

One hundred dollars will cover our costs for the muffins and for the garden.
If we charge $1.00 we will make $144.00.
If we charge $0.50 we will make $72.00. That won't be enough.
If we get some supplies donated we can lower our cost.

Maddy	flour and salt
Conor	soy milk
Bradley	oat bran
Bashir	lemon juice
Ms. Peck	vegetable oil and baking powder
Hayley	12 eggs
Markus	sugar

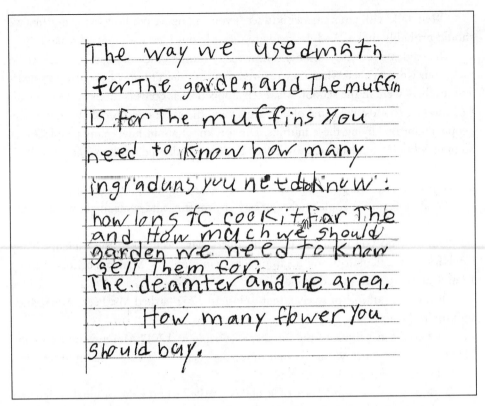

The way we used math for the garden and the muffin is for the muffins you need to know how many ingraduns you need to know: how long to cook it. For the and how much we should garden we need to know sell them for. The deamter and the area. How many flower you should bay.

Figure 4–1 *Bashir's written work summarizes what the children decided to do.*

We will only need to purchase bananas and blueberries. This brings our cost to about $20.00. This allows us to spend more money on the garden. We will charge $0.75 for the muffins. This will allow us to raise $108.00."

So, the class donated and purchased the ingredients, baked the muffins (in the kitchen at school), held their bake sale, and earned more money than they estimated they'd earn. The students planted Elizabeth's garden and even had money left over to contribute to another charity.

Ms. Peck asked them what mathematics they had used. Figure 4–2 shows what Hayley wrote.

What did these students learn? Aside from the important lessons involving "giving" and "remembering" they revisited nearly every mathematics concept and skill that they had been introduced to during the year. They got practice:

- adding and multiplying fractions

- measuring ingredients and cooking at a set temperature

- estimating and predicting costs

- determining the difference between actual cost and predicted cost

- creating a budget and deciding on pricing necessary to earn a profit

- counting mixed coins and bills to determine a quantity

"In our muffin project we used a lot of math. Hers how we did it, fist we typed a letter to Dr. Mcarthy asking if it was ok to work on the Elizabeth Garden and it was. Then we spent two making muffins, and the day after that we sold a lot got lots of money. Soon after that day Mrs. Peck went out and bought all the tools. But before that we needed to count all of the money and we had to divide, multiply, subtract, and add of course. So, Mrs. Peck bought seeds, flowers, and shovels from Home Depot. Finally we all planted them and in our success we had a lot of money left over. I sure hope to see the garden healthy and shining next year."

Figure 4–2 *Hayley explains the math that was used in the activity.*

- purchasing materials and then determining the difference between the cost and the money they had collected

- determining the area of the garden and the spacing necessary to plant seeds and plants

- determining the perimeter of the garden to purchase a plastic "fence" to go around it

- dividing up the plants so everyone had the same amount to plant

- figuring out the quantity of money remaining that could be donated to another charity

Do you think that these fifth graders realized how much mathematics went into this project? They wouldn't have without that question being posed to them, often, by their teacher. Students would have been fully involved in this project, but they wouldn't have even realized that they were doing mathematics. Ms. Peck made sure, from the very beginning, that students understood why they were working on this during mathematics class. It is likely that if these students were asked whether they use mathematics in their real lives that every one would say, "All the time!"

Making a connection, during mathematics class, to the real use of money is a wonderful way for students to get practice with computation and with measurement. Fourth and fifth graders are generally captivated by this problem:

Would you rather get an allowance of $5.00 per week, for a month, or get $0.01 on the first day of the month and then the double of this every day—during the month?

Most students who hear or see this problem think, "No way, do I want to get only $0.01 and then the double. If I get $20.00 in a four-week month that's much better." But, when students actually begin solving this problem (and it's fine to have them solve it with paper and pencil, rather than a calculator) they soon realize that within twelve days they are already earning more than $20.00. And, by the fifteenth day of that month, they will be given $163.84 (just by doubling each day). Students love this problem. It's a motivating way for them to get practice with multiplication or addition and they don't seem to mind one bit doing thirty calculations. In fact, they don't want to stop until they've doubled through the entire "month." They want to see how much money they would be getting if they did this. And, isn't this exactly what we want—for students to not want to stop practicing mathematics skills?

Money skills can also be practiced by giving students the food circulars from most every newspaper. If nutrition is also being reinforced, in science class, students can be given a specific amount of money and told that they should create a shopping list. A condition of the list, however, is that there needs to be fruits and vegetables, proteins, grains and starches, and dairy products on the list. Students can work together to create a healthy list of foods to buy with the amount of money they are given. And, certainly other conditions can be added—depending on the group of students in your class. You can tell them that they are shopping for a family of four or an elderly family. You can tell them that they are shopping for their own family (and they need to take into consideration any dietary restrictions their family might have).

Using a newspaper circular and relating this to the real use of money makes students so much more aware of the importance of learning how to be an educated consumer. In fact, coupons could be added to the lesson, and students could look for ways to reduce their cost, on specific products, by using store coupons.

Money skills can also be practiced, with fifth-grade students, by having them look at discounts in newspaper advertisements to determine the amount of savings that they would get by buying products on sale. Stores selling electronic equipment, sports equipment, and clothing have advertisements in both the newspaper and circulars that come in newspapers. Students, again, could be given a specific amount of money and told to figure out the discounted price of various items based on the discount the store is giving. And, if it's subtraction practice that you want students to get, they should be told that they need to figure out the difference between the actual price and the discounted price. Or they could figure out the difference between the discounted price and the amount of money they've been given.

One last fun thing to do with money, and intermediate students, is to bring in a jar full of saved coins. Ask students to look at the jar and estimate how much money is inside. (The jar doesn't have to be very large to have quite a bit of money in it.) Once students have estimated, ask them to write, in words, what made them think that this would be a close estimate of the value of all of the coins in the jar. (Now you also have a writing connection with the real practice of saving loose change in a jar.) When students have explained their answer in writing ask them the best way to figure out the value of all of the change. Believe me when I tell you that they will be eager to figure this out. As quarters get grouped (by fours) stop the process and let students modify their original estimate (if they want to). Do ask some students, who have made changes, to explain their thinking aloud. Finally, figure out the value and tell students how long it took you to collect all of this change. They may be motivated to try this on their own, since it's a good way to save.

Activity: How Many Weiner Dogs?

In another school, in Decatur, Alabama, Ms. Fant, the mathematics coach, posed the following question to the third-grade students she saw regularly. It was the one hundredth day and students had prepared for this big day from the first day of school. Being the dachshund lover that she is, Ms. Fant came to school wearing a lot of "weiner dog" pins. The question that she posed to the third graders in the school was,

> How many weiner dogs is Ms. Fant wearing if there are 100 weiner dog feet on her vest?

See Figure 4–3 to see what Ryan wrote.

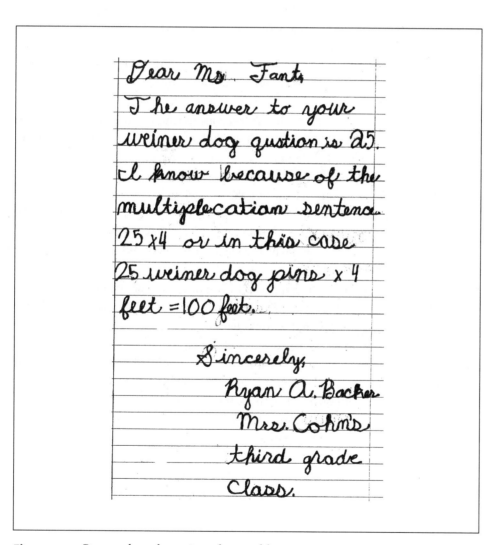

Dear Ms. Fant,
The answer to your weiner dog question is 25. I know because of the multiplecation sentence 25 x 4 or in this case 25 weiner dog pins x 4 feet =100 feet.

Sincerely,
Ryan A. Backer
Mrs. Cohn's third grade Class.

Figure 4–3 *Ryan solves the weiner dog problem.*

Motivating? Yes! And, since the day was one that was marked on the calendar from the very first day of school, it became a day rich with mathematics. Books with the theme of the one hundredth day of school were read in every classroom. Students figured out how many times they could:

■ sing Happy Birthday in 100 seconds

■ write their first and last name in 100 seconds

■ whistle a tune in 100 seconds

■ touch their toes in 100 seconds

■ read a Dr. Seuss book in 100 seconds (just to name a few things)

Teachers brainstormed ideas at different grade levels by doing a search using the descriptors: one hundredth day of school. And, something that happens in every student's life (being in school for one hundred days) became a celebration, of a sort, and a reason to practice all sorts of mathematics and language arts skills.

Telling time and figuring out elapsed time is a practical and real way to let students see how the mathematics they are learning is used every day. Why not ask students, periodically, what time it is and how many more minutes it will be before they go to: the library, the gym, or lunch? Why not have a "clock-stopper" whose role it is, during the day, to stop the class and ask someone to read the time? Practice reading an analog and digital clock is still an important skill to give to third graders, and being able to figure out how much more time it will be before the school day is over is what prompts many fifth graders to finally learn how to determine elapsed time.

Students can be given a problems like the following:

I left my home for school today at 6:15 A.M. Traffic was terrible as I crossed the bridge and it took me 57 minutes before I arrived at school. What time did I arrive?

If children believe that this really happened to you they are more willing to figure out the problem. And, when they ask, "Did that really happen?" you could say that it didn't happen this way today, but it could happen. You could also give them problems that have you stopping at the bank, dry cleaners, and grocery store on your way home from work. Give them a time when you began for home, and tell them how long you were at each place you stopped. It is likely that they will more happily tell you when you finally arrived home if they think that this really happened to you.

Time and money are easily incorporated into practical, real-life problems that help students see the usefulness of the mathematics that they are learning in school. Map reading and spatial orientation also provide this same practical application. Tell students that you are going on a trip (yes, it's a fib, but a small one). Let them know that you are hoping that you'll be able to make this trip on one tank of gasoline (and you can tell them the size of your gas tank). Give them maps and talk about the scale of the map and the average number of miles that your car gets to the gallon. Then ask them to figure out different ways that you could travel, the number of miles you'll be going, and whether you'll be able to make the trip on one tank of gasoline. For those students who know how to multiply decimals you can tell them the cost of a gallon of gas and let them figure out how much money it will cost you. Every activity that "feels real" brings students closer to the realization that mathematics is important, used often, and necessary for them to learn.

Will students get practice with the skills that they need practice with if they do projects and activities like the ones you've just read about? Of course they will! And, they'll also get to see how important it is to have these mathematics skills. There is no doubt in our minds that Ms. Peck's students realized that they needed to know so much about money, measurement, and working with fractions in order to complete their Elizabeth's Garden project. And, they approached each day's "work" with an eagerness that worksheets seldom produce.

What are some other ways that a teacher can imbed mathematics into student's real lives? Think about sporting events that students talk about in school. Whether it's an upcoming championship ball game or the Olympics, surveys can be generated that let students poll other students to see who the favored person or team might be. Surveys can also be conducted to determine what refreshments might be served at a celebratory party (for the one hundredth day of school, earning points for good behavior or a specific number of books read, or for a Thanksgiving feast).

There's no reason why a group of fourth- or fifth-grade students can't decide on how their classroom should be arranged. Grid paper can be supplied and all sorts of measurement can be taught as students work on placement of desks, areas for small-group work, and an area for the class to be together (on a rug or near the board) for full-group instruction. This could actually be done early in the academic year and then again midyear as a change is needed.

Fifth graders can learn so much more about probability and statistics if they use real data and try to make sense out of what is being shared. What does it mean when an advertisement on television says that, "Two out of three dentists prefer this toothpaste over other brands"? Having ten- and eleven-year-olds make sense out of statements like this forces them to be good consumers and helps them realize how easy it is for companies to try to trick the public. Looking for these sorts of claims in advertising gets students involved in real uses of mathematics, and gives them a reason for wanting to learn it—and not be fooled.

And, certain newspapers use graphs more regularly than others. But all newspapers use numbers (numerals and words) more often than you might think. Give students different sections of the newspaper (see Breaking News on Big Numbers in the Mathematics Connections in Everyday Experiences section on the CD) and have them figure out how many times numbers appear on a given page. Have them compare this to other sections of the newspaper and then speculate about why certain sections of the paper use numbers more than other sections. Have them look to see if the numbers are "actual" numbers or estimates. Does the paper report that 18,546 people attended the baseball game, or 18,000? These afford you an opportunity to talk about the real use of "rounded" numbers.

Almanacs and different books with facts provide students with athletes' "records," CEOs' salaries, rivers' lengths across the world, and other information that will give them practice with decimals, large numbers, and money. When a newspaper prints that the new national debt is $8 trillion does the public really know what this means?

We know that we don't have a clue how huge that amount really is. But, trying to collect even a million of something (or counting the quantity of kidney beans in a bag and then figuring out how many bags would give a person one million of them) would give a student some sense of the enormity of this number. Then, knowing that one thousand times this number would be a billion, and one thousand times that would be a trillion really does help students "see" how big the debt would be. And, then speculating about the number of nickels or quarters that this would be (and deciding what the weight would be in ounces) gives fifth graders a realistic sense of weight.

The Cartesian Product for multiplication takes on true meaning when students are given four different shirts and five different pairs of pants and asked, "What are all of the different shirt/pants outfits that can be made using these clothes?"

Not only will students determine all of the outfits, but they could write about which outfit they prefer and why. And, when asked to represent this on a sheet of white paper it is likely that students would not need a lot of direction to draw each of the possibilities. And, isn't this a fairly realistic way to think about ordered pairs or the combinations model for multiplication? Teachers could pose this as a question and leave the strategies for solving this up to students.

Stuart Murphy's (2004) book *Divide and Ride* is a great way to springboard into the real uses of division. Friends go to an amusement park to go on a variety of rides. But, many of these rides require a specific number of people to a seat. With each ride the friends divide, see the remainders, and figure out how many new people need to be seated with them in order for the ride to begin. Problems like this occur all of the time and create a real context for the need to know how to compute and think mathematically.

What are some other ways to connect mathematics to the real world? In a diverse school family members can come into the classroom to share games that involve mathematical thinking, tapestries that are commonly found, baskets that are woven, and coins and currency that are used in the country of their origin. Third- through fifth-grade students are fascinated to learn about the different climates in a foreign country and then to compare these to the climate in their own state. And, a discussion of temperature often brings up the point that the United States uses temperatures measured in degrees Fahrenheit, while most other places in the world measure temperature in degrees Celsius. If asked, "Is it hot, warm, cool, or cold if you hear that it is 27 degrees Celsius in December, in Brisbane, Australia?" most students will relate this to what they know about the temperature, in December, where they live. Thinking about other cultures and other countries not only gives students a different, more global perspective but gives them practice making sense out of temperature.

Lastly, every experience where mathematics is being used regularly (whether it's to measure and then build something, balance a budget, figure out the price of an item that's been reduced 20 percent, or determine the fairness of a game) gives older students incentives for learning mathematics. They see it being used, not just in school (during mathematics class), but in the real world—every day, throughout the day.

We have found that while many newer textbooks do have a better variety of story problems for students to solve, they often do not have specific types of problems that might interest your students. How could they know that in your community soccer is "the" sport that students follow? The statistics of these athletes would be more important to your students than those of basketball players. It's very helpful to generate story problems based on the interests of your students. The students are more invested in solving problems that make sense to them, rather than to some "average" student from inside their textbook. And, it's worth your time to generate these problems using the names of students in your class. Again, this keeps students motivated and interested in doing mathematics.

Questions for Discussion

1. How are you already relating real-life situations to your mathematics classroom?

2. What are some concepts that give students difficulties, and how could these be connected to real-life situations that could make them more real?

3. What holidays or events are coming up that could be used to generate story problems or problem situations?

4. What community figures might be called upon to provide students with information about how they use mathematics in the jobs that they do?

CHAPTER 5

Assessment of the Connections Standard

As an integral part of mathematics instruction, assessment contributes significantly to all students' learning. Because students learn mathematics while being assessed, assessments are learning opportunities as well as opportunities for students to demonstrate what they know and can do.

—National Council of Teachers of Mathematics,
Assessment Standards for School Mathematics

Defining Assessment

It's the first day of school following a restful winter break. Sure, some students will need to be reminded that vacation is over and it's time to settle back into the routine of being in school, but the majority of students seem happy to be back. They like school. They like seeing their friends, and they enjoy the interesting, exciting activities that they get to do each day. What they don't know, however, is what's in store for them in math class—preparation, every day, for the state-mandated assessment. And what they also don't know is that their teachers dislike this test preparation almost as much as they do.

In some classrooms, schools, and even school systems instruction seems to cease as teachers prepare their students for the state test. And, this test may be given as early as March causing some teachers to believe that they were supposed to have "covered" the curriculum by the time they are to give this assessment.

Is this really what we are supposed to be doing? Are students supposed to learn a year's worth of content by the time they go on their winter break? If, by some miracle they do learn everything by the end of December, what are they supposed to be learning once the state assessment is over? And, is this really what assessment is supposed to be anyway? Is assessment only the last step of the instructional process?

The *Assessment Standards* tells us that classroom assessment should—

- provide a rich variety of mathematical topics and problem situations

- give students opportunities to investigate problems in many ways

- question and listen to students

- look for evidence of learning from many sources

- expect students to use concepts and procedures effectively in solving problems (NCTM 1995, 2)

Nowhere in this list, describing what assessment should be, is the statement that all instruction should come to an end in order to prepare students for a single test that is given by the state.

Well sure, you may be thinking, but this list of goals was written before high-stakes testing came along. You also may be wondering who the idealist was who wrote this list. We all know that it was developed before the No Child Left Behind Act. And teachers, principals, schools, and districts do seem to feel a great deal of stress that the funding they will get from the federal government is directly correlated with how well their students do on the state assessment. It's no wonder that tensions run high as teachers and principals fret over what should be done to ensure that students demonstrate high achievement.

The *Assessment Standards* were developed and disseminated in 1995, and this was before many states had mandated yearly testing of all students in third through eighth grade. But is this state measure of accountability meant to be the only factor that drives instruction?

We believe that students should not have their instruction limited because of a single assessment, nor should assessment be viewed as one single test. As important as the state assessment may be (and it is a piece of information that can be used to better understand what it is a student, or a group of students know), it isn't meant to be the only means for determining this information. Let's look at what assessment should be and see how making connections can positively impact what you know about students' understanding of mathematics.

What Is Assessment?

"As teachers, we get what we ask for. If we ask only for simple numerical answers, students will value only procedures and computational tasks. But, if we ask for discussion, explanation and elaboration, and if we reward these kinds of answers, then students will value understanding and meaning" (Higgins 1988).

Assessment provides us with a means for better understanding what it is our students know, and do not know. And, there's got to be a balance between the correct (or incorrect) answer and some means for explaining what was done to get this answer. Both the process or strategy used to derive an answer, and the actual answer, itself, is important for a teacher to see.

In NCTM's 1993 Yearbook, *Assessment in the Mathematics Classroom*, Norman L. Webb defines assessment as "the comprehensive accounting of a student's or group of students' knowledge." He goes on to say that assessment helps teachers make instructional decisions based on information provided and that it should not be "the end of educational experiences; instead, it is a means to achieve educational goals" (NCTM 1993, 1). Bright and Joyner write, "The importance of teachers being able to assess where their students are cannot be emphasized too strongly. Teachers must understand the strengths and areas of need of their students in order to help students achieve" (1998, IX). Webb's quote, as well as this one, defines classroom assessment. This information gathering, or formative assessment, allows teachers to observe students and collect work samples in order to make instructional decisions. "Formative assessment is the ongoing and often informal evaluation that takes place during the teaching–learning process. It enables teachers to monitor the day-to-day progress of students and to plan the next teaching phase" (Irons, Rowan, Bamberger and Suarez 1998, 97).

This is different from summative assessment, which is more like the test that is given by the state at some specific point in the academic year. We'll separate the two and talk about formative assessment and mathematics connections. Later we'll look at how making these connections can actually save you time and make that state or national (summative) assessment seem less foreboding.

Formative or Ongoing Assessment

Think about the following problem (also see CDs for Sale in the Planning and Assessment section on the CD):

> **A CD costs $14.99. The sign says, "SALE 30% off the regular price or buy two at the regular price and get the third one for free."**

You ask students to figure out which way of buying CDs is better than the other if they wanted to purchase three CDs. Their assignment is to figure this out and then be ready to defend their findings.

As students pull out their calculators and paper and pencil you overhear them talking. You can hear a student say that he's "seen stuff like this at stores and he never knows which would be a better deal. You feel like you'll be ripped off if you don't say the right thing," he tells his classmates. As their teacher you now know that they are making a connection between their real world and the world of mathematics in their classroom. This is good. And, as they proceed to figure out the answer, they will be making a connection among mathematics concepts and skills as they solve this problem. It is likely that they will:

- round $14.99 to $15.00 (for ease in computing)

- multiply 70 percent times $15.00 to determine the cost of a single discounted CD

- multiply $10.50 (the cost of one CD) by 3 to determine the cost of three CDs

- double $14.99 or add $15.00 to itself

- subtract $30.00 (two CDs with one free) from $31.50 (30% off of each CD) to determine the savings

Since they will be asked to defend their answer, it is also possible that these fifth graders will be asked to write out their reason for choosing the "buy two get one free" deal. Another connection is then made between writing and mathematics.

This sort of problem-solving scenario could be used as both a formative and summative assessment. If you've been studying percent this problem could definitely give you information about the strategies that students are using to determine cost. Based on what students do to solve the problem you could make a decision about how to proceed in the teaching of percent ideas. This sort of assessment also lets you see other skills that a student may have. Do students take shortcuts or find ways to think differently about numbers? If no calculator is given, do they compute with accuracy in an efficient manner? Does their answer make sense to them and are they able to defend what they've done to arrive at it? These are all things that you need to be thinking about as you come up with good tasks that connect mathematics ideas.

How is this sort of performance-based task beneficial to you, and to your students? It saves you time. By creating a task that assesses a variety of skills, at the same time (rather than assessing isolated skills—one at a time) you are giving yourself additional time to introduce and reinforce new concepts and skills. The benefit to students is that they see the usefulness of the mathematics they are learning. They can use the skills they're learning when they read through advertisements in newspapers and when they shop.

What are performance-based assessments? Often they involve giving a student, or a small group of students, a mathematical task that may take "from half an hour to several days to complete or solve" (Stenmark 1989, 26). The teacher often asks questions of students as they work on these tasks, which often involve writing or are connected to other subject areas.

Observing and questioning are powerful assessment tools. As elementary math learners we recall sitting quietly in class and completing sheets of practice problems or copying problems right out of our textbook onto loose-leaf paper. Our teacher usually remained at her desk, probably correcting the homework papers that we had just turned in. Interaction with the teacher was often limited to a reprimand for inappropriate behavior or a reminder to read the directions carefully. Fortunately, mathematics education has come a long way from our personal experiences. Mathematics classrooms today look and sound very different. Students are interacting with one another and with the teacher. The teacher may be working with a small group of students or moving around the classroom to observe what students are doing and ask questions that might facilitate learning. The discourse that occurs at this time is a valuable assessment tool.

CLASSROOM-TESTED TIP

Many teachers find it difficult to remember what it is that they observe as they walk around the room during problem-solving tasks. They question students, but then forget what they've heard or forget who they've questioned. Keeping a record of what's been seen and heard is important in documenting and assessing. We've found that using address labels gives us just enough space to record some observations and notes, but isn't terribly overwhelming to keep up with. Here's how we do this. We take a blank sheet of address labels and print out our class list (one student per label). Then, as we walk around the room we write the date on the label and write a few notes about what we hear and see. Once mathematics is over (or at the end of the school day), we peel off each label that's been written on. We have a page, or several, in a loose-leaf notebook, for each student in the class. The written label is stuck onto this page beneath the label previously placed. This gives us an ongoing record of things we've heard and seen during mathematics class. This information can be used when meeting with families, during conferences, or it can be used (along with other pieces of information) to document grades given on report cards. Usually we can observe six to eight students during the time that they are working on a problem, which means notes are placed on student's pages at least twice a week.

Activity: Naming and Stating the Value of 3.54

Let's look at the interactions that took place in Mr. Curtis' fourth-grade classroom during a simple exercise in which he asked students to name and state the value of 3.54. This simple task could be linked to ideas of place value, decimals, money, number and operations, and even equivalencies. The connections within and among mathematics concepts provide options to the teacher when determining the context, materials, and format for instruction and assessment.

Mr. Curtis asked his fourth-grade students to name the value of the quantity and describe a situation when such a quantity might be used (see What's 3.54? in the Planning and Assessment section on the CD).

Lydia recorded that the quantity was "three point five four" and that you might "see this number when counting money." Mr. Curtis questioned her more about the way she had named this value. He commented that people "do often read decimals this way, but that mathematicians usually say decimals another way."

Sylvia responded with, "Oh, I mean three and fifty-four hundredths."

Mr. Curtis let her know that this was exactly how mathematicians read decimal numbers, and she looked pleased when she heard this. Then he asked a question that seemed to puzzle her. "How big is fifty-four hundredths, Sylvia?" She gave him the look that suggested that she really wasn't sure what he meant. And, she responded with, "I don't know."

Now comes the challenge to any teacher. What do you do with an "I don't know" situation? Do you call on another student to help her out, to tell her the answer, so she now knows, or ask her another question or direct her thinking with some statement that will let her come up with some meaningful connection? If you chose the third option, you were right. Let's see what Mr. Curtis did.

It was clear that Mr. Curtis had been practicing his reflecting and questioning because he then said, "Remember that you wrote that a number like this could be an amount of money? How much money would fifty-four hundredths be?"

Sylvia responded by saying that it would be fifty-four cents.

"And how much is that in relation to a dollar?" Mr. Curtis continued.

"It's a little bit more than a half dollar. That's just fifty cents," Sylvia continued.

"OK, so let's think about this in relation to the decimal 3.54," said Mr. Curtis.

"I see," Sylvia said. "The fraction part, I mean the decimal part is a little bit more than one-half."

"Well, what if we found a string and when we measured it we found that it was three and fifty-four hundredths of a meter," Mr. Curtis now asked.

"The string would be about three and a half meters long. Right! This decimal is about three and a half," Sylvia announced confidently.

What had Mr. Curtis done during this diagnostic interview (which, by the way, took place during class time while others were listening and preparing to be asked questions, too)? He used what Sylvia already seemed to know (that decimals could be connected to money), to help her make a connection to the approximate size of this particular decimal. It was through his questioning that Mr. Curtis helped Sylvia build on and extend her current level of understanding.

Could Mr. Curtis have simply told Sylvia that fifty-four hundredths was close to one-half? Of course he could have. And, it would have been faster than asking her questions. But, with his questioning he was able to lead Sylvia to the next level of understanding. And, once there he posed the next question to her, to confirm that she was indeed making this connection. When he asked her about the string he was assessing whether she was able to synthesize what she had just said and apply this understanding to a completely different situation. And, this particular teacher does this sort of thing all of the time. He seeks opportunities for such student empowerment through classroom observations and questioning. (See Questions About Connections in the Planning and Assessment section on the CD, which is a list of questions applicable to helping students identify connections in mathematics.)

Students offer a multitude of clues to every teacher who is working on understanding their strengths and area of weakness. They include written work samples, the questions that they ask (of the teacher and other students), the level of persistence and intuitiveness demonstrated when solving a problem, and "the look" that reveals a degree of satisfaction, contentment, or puzzlement or frustration. It was both "the look" and Sylvia's inability to make sense out of what she had just said that led Mr. Curtis to continue questioning her until she made a connection that made sense to her.

Part of our job as teachers is to interpret all of these clues and transform them into smart and informed instructional decisions. And, connections play a vital role in the transformation process. The connections that exist in mathematics foster the construction of knowledge. As teachers, we can use connections to steer this process by asking ourselves:

- How might the concept relate to another concept that we have already studied?

- What are the prerequisite skills that my students already have that will make these new skills easier for them to learn?

- Is there a way to reinforce these concepts and skills in other areas of my curriculum?

- What are the real-world applications for this mathematical idea that I can draw upon to make this more real to my students?

An analysis of these potential connections can offer you strategies and a means for directing your instruction so that students may advance from their current understandings to new, more complex ones. NCTM notes that, "Assessment is thus an important tool for understanding the knowledge that students are constructing, the meanings that they are assigning to mathematical ideas, and the progress that they are making toward achieving mathematical power" (1993, 2).

If we begin each day with some daily number sense activity we can often assess the growth in number sense from early in the year until later in the year. Many of our classrooms have students generate equations for which the answer is the number of days they have been in school. It's easy to make some assumptions about what a student knows if each day, for the first several weeks of school, their equation remains "1 + 1 + 1 + 1 + 1. . . ." This means of ongoing assessment may give us a glimpse into how comfortable a student is with his or her own understanding of equations, as well as the level of sophistication of his or her response. What you say to a student who continues to do this (whether the student is in third, fourth, or fifth grade) may make a difference as to whether they take a risk in the near future and try a different type of equation.

Sharing ideas through discourse often provides you with just the vehicle for challenging the timid or reticent student as well as giving him or her ideas. We learn so much from our students during these brief, opening activities. The following are some of the responses we got, early in the year, from fourth-grade students. It was the twenty-first day of school (only seventy-nine more days until the hundredth day), and students were asked to come up with three different equations where twenty-one would be the answer. Students knew that they'd get to share at least one of their equations (since this was the routine each day). So, they often picked the "hardest" one to share. In some ways this had become a bit of a competition. All the while the teacher was making notes about what these equations told her about her student's number sense and level of understanding of computation.

Several students at a time came forward to write their equations:

$$3 \times 7 = 21 \quad 100 - 79 = 21 \quad 1 + 20 = 21 \quad 3 \times 10 - 9 = 21$$
$$81 \div 9 + 3 \times 2 - 3 = 21 \quad 16 + 5 = 21 \quad 3(2 + 5) = 21 \quad 11 + 11 \times 1 - 1 = 21$$

Are all of these correct? Does each produce the answer of 21? No, and neither did some of the other equations that were written. So, if the object of this activity is to do a quick assessment, each day of number sense and computational proficiency, what does the teacher need to do with this information?

Here's what this teacher did. She asked the girl who had written $3 \times 10 - 9 = 21$ to explain how she knew that this was the right answer. Emily explained that first she multiplied the 3 times the 10 and that equaled 30. Then she thought that 30 minus 9 equaled 21. Her teacher responded with this statement, "Your equation is correct and it follows a rule that mathematicians use when they have a lot of different operations in an equation. Mathematicians decided that no matter where they appear in an equation you need to multiply and divide before you add and subtract. Let's see if this is what Emily did." And the others in the class did just that. They looked to confirm that Emily had followed this "mathematician's rule." The teacher then asked whether there were other equations on the white board that had different operations. Ms. Wallace said, "Let's see if our new 'mathematician's rule' was used by the people who wrote these equations." Without focusing on the student who had incorrectly written the class then tried this "rule" as they solved $81 \div 9 + 3 \times 2 - 3 = 21$.

Patrick first asked this question (and it's one that we hear a lot from fifth- and even sixth-grade students), "Are you supposed to multiply first and then divide before you add and subtract, or just multiply or divide before you add or subtract?"

Ms. Wallace smiled as she repeated this new "mathematician's rule." She told them that mathematicians felt that you could either multiply or divide before adding or subtracting. She asked Patrick whether this made sense to him and he responded with, "Cool, I just needed to know whether I was supposed to go into the middle and multiply that 3 times the 2 before I divided the 81 by 9."

"The answer is supposed to be 12," Rachel announced, after Ms. Wallace gave these students about a minute to work on this equation. Several other students signaled that they had gotten that answer as well.

"How did you figure this out?" Ms. Wallace asked Rachel.

"See, the first thing that I did was divide 81 by 9 and that equals 9—right? Then I multiplied the 3 times the 2 and that equals 6. Next I added the 6 and the 9 and that equals 15. When you subtract 3 from 15 that equals 12. So the answer is 12, not 21."

Ms. Wallace's next comment allowed the class to decide what to do with the equation that was currently on the board. She said, "So, what should we do with this equation?" And, the class (nearly in unison) said, "Erase it." No one student was singled out as being correct or incorrect and the class learned something important about the order of the operations.

Did Ms. Wallace make a mental note about who had originally written the equation incorrectly? She sure did, and then she recorded it on the loose-leaf page where she had this student's address label notes. And, it was likely that she'd find a time to make sure that this student understood what had transpired during this activity.

Having students talk about and write about what they know and how they know things is an essential part of mathematics today. "Communication in mathematics has become important as we move into an era of a 'thinking' curriculum. Students are urged to discuss ideas with each other, to ask questions, to diagram and graph problem situations for clarity. Writing in mathematics classes, once rare, are now vital" (EQUALS 1989, 11). This writing takes on many forms. Making journal entries, explaining the process or strategy used to solve a problem, responding to both open-ended or specific questions, and summarizing what's been learned during the week allows a teacher to see a student's thinking.

And writing affords students some time to reflect on a lesson and summarize the key components of a concept. Once relegated to language arts lesson only, writing is now a key component both in lessons and in assessments.

Activity: Comparing Fractions

After a lesson on comparing fractions, Ms. Jones put the following question on the board and instructed students to respond in their journal (see Comparing Fractions in the Planning and Assessment section on the CD):

> Which value is greater, $\frac{3}{4}$ or $\frac{4}{6}$? Use words and illustrations to explain your answer.

Thomas' journal response revealed to Ms. Jones that he was able to use familiar benchmarks when comparing fractions. He described his strategy as one of looking at the denominators and stated that fourths are larger than sixths. He did add, "But there are also more sixths, so I can't use the denominator to decide." He proceeded by showing how the two fractions compared to $\frac{1}{2}$. (See Figure 5–1.)

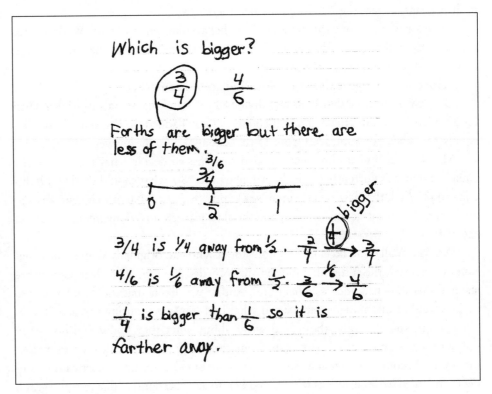

Figure 5–1 *Thomas' comparison of the two fractions*

His work shows that $\frac{3}{4}$ is $\frac{1}{4}$ larger than $\frac{1}{2}$ and that $\frac{4}{6}$ is $\frac{1}{6}$ bigger than $\frac{1}{2}$. So he concludes that $\frac{3}{4}$ is bigger since $\frac{1}{4}$ is bigger than $\frac{1}{6}$. (If Ms. Jones had just asked for an answer she would have never "heard" the thinking strategy that Thomas employed to solve this problem.)

As she analyzes Thomas' journal entry, Ms. Jones verifies his ability to compare two fractions using concepts of addition, subtraction (or decomposition of a fraction), equivalence, and then to represent the region model successfully. He used no "formal" procedure to find a common denominator, but his understanding of the relative magnitude of common fractions was keen and his ability to connect what he already knew to explain this new situation was clear.

Constructed Response Versus Selected Response Items

Because selected response or multiple choice items are easier to score and probably less expensive to score, they are often used on summative assessments. It's unusual for a state assessment to have only constructed response items, where students write to explain their answer or illustrate to show their strategy. But, selecting an answer from a list of provided choices is less informative for teachers and less effective in formative assessments. When students provide the answer and the process they used to find this answer, you have a much clearer picture of what this learner knows and understands. A constructed response item offers much more information, which translates into more effective planning and adjustments in instruction. Nahrgang and Peterson (1986, 461) explain that "writing enhances learning by giving students the opportunity to formulate, organize, internalize, and evaluate" concepts. And a student's writing provides a teacher with a much clearer understanding of what a student really knows.

The following are some ideas (for each of NCTM's content standards) for connecting assessments with writing:

- *Number and Operation:* Provide students with a numerical expression, something as simple as 352 + 869 = , and ask them to solve this in two different ways and explain their strategies.

- *Algebra:* Provide students with the following problem and have them explain the strategy that they used to solve this, as well as the rule for knowing what the outcome would be. (*Example:* To make a certain shade of pink a paint shop puts in 2 squirts of white for every 1 squirt of pink. How many squirts of pink would be required if 12 squirts of pink are in the paint can?)

- *Geometry:* Give each student two different plane or solid figures and ask them to list the attributes that they have in common as well as those that are different.

- *Measurement:* Give students a rectangle (drawn on grid paper) where part of the figure is hidden. Have them determine the area of this and explain how they got their answer.

■ *Probability and Data Analysis:* Give students the following information:

A bag holds 10 blocks. There are 3 colors of cubes inside. After 20 trials, where a block is taken out and then put back inside, these are the findings: red blocks—13, blue blocks—5, white blocks—2. Use this information to predict what is inside the bag and explain how you arrived at this answer.

Concept Maps

It is worth mentioning again that students often do view school mathematics as something completely different from the mathematics that they might use in their daily living. These connections are often implicit and assumed by adults, but are far less obvious to students. It is our role to help students recognize that mathematics is necessary in the real world. Then, they are learning it not just to pass some test, but to be able to use it in their lives.

Mrs. Prama assessed her students' awareness of mathematics used in life situations by assigning concept maps. Concept maps are graphic organizers, created by students, to highlight the mathematics used in specific situations. Mrs. Prama first assigned each group of four students to choose an event or common activity experienced by many people. The class brainstormed a list of ideas, which included:

■ going on vacation

■ planning a party

■ building a doghouse

■ moving into a new house

■ buying school supplies or clothes to go back to school

■ participating in a sporting event

Each group took a different event and recorded the name on a blank sheet of paper. Mrs. Prama instructed the groups of students to first talk about and then record all of the necessary types of mathematics required to participate in their activity. Her only specific direction in format was that ideas that related to one another had to be connected in some way on their diagram.

The students worked in their small groups for about thirty minutes. One particular group mapped the mathematics used when planning a birthday party (see Figure 5–2).

They recorded six different concepts of mathematics and provided specific examples related to the party. The group's final reflection of their work was very revealing to Mrs. Prama.

Alex pointed to their concept map and said that everything on it pointed to something else. Robin replied with, "Yeah, and so many things point to decimals. We really need to know about decimals!"

Teddy said, "It's like planning a birthday party is really a math lesson!"

The students definitely made the connection between mathematics and the real world. They recognized the utility of learning to multiply money, learn fractional

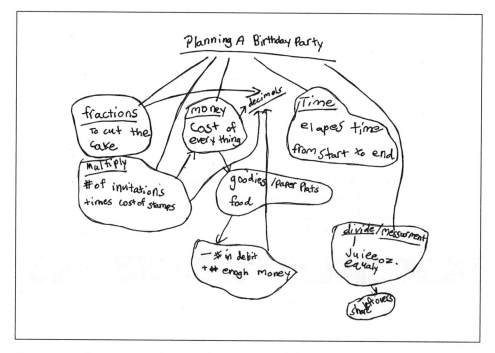

Figure 5–2 *Concepts used when planning a birthday party*

parts of a region, and divide ounces. Teddy's statement was a priceless. Could a teacher want anything more?

Mrs. Prama now understood so much more about what her students knew about the ways that mathematics related to their lives. By conducting this assessment she is able to make future instructional decisions.

Portfolios

Colleges of education often require that preservice teachers create a portfolio that can be used as they interview for teaching positions. This collection of artifacts not only demonstrates what a student knows but offers some insight into what is valued. The same thing holds true for portfolios of your students' work. These can be used to showcase growth over time, based on the projects and papers saved throughout the year. Papers and projects saved help you communicate more effectively with families about their children's work, and help you collaborate with colleagues about your instructional program. For students in the intermediate grades portfolios give them some "say" as to what should be kept to represent their understanding of mathematics concepts and skills. An assessment portfolio may help them see mathematical connections, as well as be a means for self-assessment. Inside the portfolio should be the following things:

- Samples of student work from throughout the school year: early, middle, and late. The sample could be the same question asked, and answered, over time. For example, "What is multiplication?"

■ Written samples to an open-ended question that demonstrates individual understanding. For example, "What do you know about probability?"

■ A report, based on an investigation, that demonstrates individual as well as group understanding of a concept or skill. For example,

Name two numbers that are larger than 12 that when multiplied together produce a product that is between 700 and 1,000. Explain how you got your answer.

Other artifacts can be selected by you or by your students, but the goal of the portfolio is to help you and your students see how progress has been made and how connections throughout the year have aided in this growth.

CLASSROOM-TESTED TIP

Using a portfolio may seem overwhelming to you as you try to get organized and figure out what's worth saving versus what can be sent home or even discarded. We have found that having either an accordion file or a storage crate makes the collection of student work more manageable. Each student gets to decorate their portfolio folder and at the end of each week artifacts are either removed or added to the folder. Students in grades 3 through 5 can be made responsible for seeing that papers and projects are neatly inside and that the examples of work represent their growth over time.

Creating Effective Assessments

Catalogs are filled with assessment materials. There is no shortage of publishers willing to provide you with quizzes, constructed response items, and even journal ideas. But do the companies that create these materials really know your students? And do you really have time to be looking through catalogs to find these items? It almost takes less time to create the resources that assess the essence of what students know and have learned. If you keep the following things in mind you will create tools that are effective and efficient and that accurately gauge your student's understandings. Consider the following questions when designing and implementing a formative assessment:

Content:	What is the concept or skill I'm assessing?
	What are the foundational skills required for success?
	How are prior units of study related to this new concept?
	What types of questions or problems will adequately assess the content?
Format:	How much content am I going to assess?
	Are students likely to respond with words or other representations?

How much class time can be devoted to this assessment?

Is this a pre- or postassessment?

How quickly would I like to be able to interpret the results and give feedback to my students?

Scoring: What tool will I use to score the items?

How will the scores be communicated to students?

Are students aware of the criteria for success?

Will students have an opportunity to repeat this task if they aren't satisfied with their performance?

Standard for Success: What is the standard for proficiency?

How will I address instruction for those not meeting this standard?

What is the next step for students who do or don't meet this standard?

How will I monitor performance?

Monitoring Performance

Have you ever had so many piles of papers on your desk that you don't even know what's there anymore? Collecting formative assessment data, on a regular basis, compounds this problem. Yet an effective system for monitoring student performance gives us useable and important information. The Classroom-Tested Tip of recording "snippets" of information on an address label can help you quickly organize what students understand as they work in class.

A peek into Ms. Taylor's notebook reveals these statements:

A.J. multiplies 2-digit by 2-digit without error.

D.L. has difficulty with regrouping when multiplying 2-digit by 2-digit. May need to write out entire partial product.

V.S. seems confused when a zero is in the tens place of a 3-digit by 2-digit problem.

B.D. completed all examples quickly and correctly, needs extensions.

These comments are just notes, made to herself, which gives Ms. Taylor some direction to move in with her students. She can pinpoint their needs and even create some small groups for future instruction.

Using some sort of rubric is another popular method for monitoring student progress and performance. A rubric is a scale that outlines the specific criteria for attaining each possible score. This is a different approach to scoring from what we likely experienced as learners. Traditionally, answers were either right or wrong. Rubrics help to identify the in-between of right and wrong. A well-defined rubric shows the progression from lower levels of performance to high levels of performance and provides a sequence to guide students in attaining the next level.

The most effective rubrics are those designed according to a specific task; be sure to share this with students prior to their completing the assignment. If students have the criteria in mind while engaging in the activity, they are more likely to consider this as they work. Additionally, student use of rubrics to revisit and refine their work seems to boost performance.

As teachers, we "house" the data we collect regarding student performance. It is on our desks, in our minds, and in our notebooks. We record, analyze, and interpret the data to inform instruction. We are doing a lot of monitoring and record a lot of information. What should our students be doing? Where do they fit in this process? After all, this data is all about them. Ms. Brown considered this question and implemented the practice of student data books. The students record much of the same data she records. The data books are accessible to the students at all times and are labeled with covers designed by each individual. The books are subdivided and include a section for each subject. The section designated for mathematics contains a line graph of basic fact quiz results, a grid to record unit test scores, a calendar colored to highlight completed homework assignments, a list of "successes" and "still needs some attention," and goals for the next marking period. Ms. Brown has shared the job of monitoring student performance with her students.

The decision to do this came about because of frustration that she felt when she overhead students saying, "She gave me a 2." Ms. Brown wanted her students to understand that she was not giving them anything. It was the score they earned. Data books seemed like a good possible solution. And when asked she explained that their perspectives changed. Her students became more responsible and invested in their learning. They began seeing that their effort paid off and they felt more in control of how they performed.

Providing Feedback

An integral part of the teaching and learning process is to provide feedback to students about their performance. "Academic feedback is more strongly and consistently related to achievement than any other teaching behavior. This relationship is consistent regardless of grade, socioeconomic status, race or school setting" (Bellon, Bellon, and Blank 1992). Feedback was essentially what Ms. Brown was providing to her students through the data books, a form of evaluative feedback. The students were tracking their performance and setting goals for future performance. As teachers we also need to provide descriptive feedback (Davies 2000). Descriptive feedback is specific to the task or standard. It differs from praise, which is more of a value judgment about the learner. Feedback is about the work and the performance, not the person. Effective feedback gives specific information. An example of effective feedback would be, "Your response that $28 \div 6 = 4r4$ does not answer the question, which was *How many vans are required for the field trip?*"

Feedback lets the student know exactly where he or she stands and is specific enough to give some direction for their next steps. It is a necessary component of instruction and assessment because it allows students to make adjustments while they are learning, and to use the information in future attempts.

Ongoing assessment and effective feedback are powerful tools in helping students make necessary connections and learn mathematics. As educators, we have to consider our students where they are and where they need to go. Sometimes, as we find ourselves plugging away we ask ourselves: "Would my instruction look any different if the room was empty?" What exactly does this mean? Well, if we're moving from indicator to indicator to "complete" the curriculum, placing pacing and content as a priority, it doesn't really matter who is sitting in the classroom. Tomorrow's lesson will be tomorrow's lesson regardless of what happened today. But when we consider who our learners are and continually assess student understanding, this information guides us to the direction we'll be taking tomorrow and in the future.

Summing It Up

You know the expression, "Time flies when you're having fun!" Time does fly by in the average classroom. When teachers connect mathematics concepts and skills across the curriculum assessment ideas can be combined as well. And even though the time is flying by, students are learning a good deal more content because of these connections. Remember that during a social studies unit you can certainly assess map-reading skills (noting who understands scale drawings and who can determine the distance from one city to another). In science, as plants begin growing students can be assessed on their ability to accurately measure. Why not "check this off" your list of things to assess in mathematics if it can be done during another unit of study?

And, when you carefully combine mathematics content across the curriculum, you get more accomplished, and assess many different levels of understanding. You may have to develop these assessments because your textbook or program may be looking at only the skill from one chapter. But, it will be worth your while to do this, especially if you are developing the kinds of lessons that make connections among and within mathematics concepts and between mathematics and other areas of the curriculum.

CLASSROOM-TESTED TIP

Students offer a variety of strategies and perspectives when solving problems. As a facilitator to this process, the teacher often poses questions and initiates dialogue with students while they solve problems. Many times, a student will share an idea that the entire class should hear and reflect on. However, we may choose to delay the sharing time rather than interrupt students in the middle of a problem. One strategy is to ask students to record the statement or strategy on a 3-inch by 5-inch sticky note and place it on the chalkboard at the front of the room. When there is time for discussion, the student and the teacher will be reminded of the important point or strategy. A piece of chart paper labeled "Points to Ponder" can serve as a permanent display for this ongoing practice. As points are discussed, the notes are removed. Students enjoy having their ideas posted and placed on an agenda for group discussion and sharing. Even if all of the points are not discussed, the student feels like his work was recognized by the teacher and his peers.

CLASSROOM-TESTED TIP

The assessment process should not be carried out solely by the teacher. It is our responsibility to teach students to measure their own level of understanding. Engaging students in the assessment process empowers them with the knowledge of understanding where they are in comparison to where they need to be. Allow students to score sample papers (anonymous ones) according to a specific scale, such as a rubric (see Scoring Rubric: How Did I Do? in the Planning and Assessment section on the CD). Provide examples of work at all levels of proficiency. One quick method for collecting student work samples is to choose a task with a colleague, administer the task to both classes, and then swap papers. After a few samples, students become rather accurate in scoring the samples. The class discussion during this process helps to clarify for students the components of each score, and provides a comparison for students when considering their own work. We might think that students would inflate their scores, when in reality they are often more critical of their own work.

Questions for Discussion

1. What should students know and be able to demonstrate?

2. Which formats of assessment have you used and found most effective when analyzing student work and planning for instruction?

3. How are your students involved in monitoring their own learning and setting goals for future performance?

4. What kind of feedback is most effective in boosting achievement?

CHAPTER 6

Connections Across the Content Standards

When students can connect mathematical ideas, their understanding is deeper and more lasting. They can see mathematical connections in the rich interplay among mathematical topics, in contexts that relate mathematics to other subjects and in their own interests and experiences.

—National Council of Teachers of Mathematics, *Principles and Standards of School Mathematics*

You have been given a rationale for making connections within mathematics strands, among mathematics standards, and between mathematics and other content areas or with real-life experiences. In addition, you've been given activities, tested out in different classrooms, that helped students make sense out of the mathematics concepts and skills that were being introduced or reinforced. These activities varied across the NCTM's content standards, so it was easier for you to see how making these connections could be done—regardless of the content that was being taught.

While making and recognizing connections is a critical process when exploring mathematics concepts and skills, it is just one of the five process standards discussed in the NCTM *Standards*. These include problem solving, reasoning and proof, communication, connections, and representations. In a standards-based lesson these process standards are intertwined within the instruction. Recognizing and making connections are often achieved through some problem-solving experience. Students are often asked to justify their answers, use reasoning skills to make inferences, choose effective strategies, and hypothesize whether a solution will "always" work as they solve problems. They also communicate their ideas both verbally and in writing. And, either through a manipulative model, some illustration, or some symbolic solution students represent what it is they know. These five process standards often interconnect in an effective mathematics classroom.

The process standards help to define the way it is we teach, while the content standards serve as the driving force in identifying what we teach. Both work simultaneously to enhance instruction and facilitate learning.

This chapter gives you specific suggestions for ways to make connections with each of the five content standards. It is the interconnectedness of the content and process standards through sample classroom lessons that is the key. Each section summarizes the content, describes an activity linking the content through connections, and finishes with a discussion of the mathematics involved. Activities are discussed and ways to differentiate them are elaborated upon. In this way you will be able to see how the activity might be done with third graders who are quite capable with mathematics ideas, as well as those who may need additional time. And, we'll provide you with activities that could also be done with fourth- and fifth-grade students as well. This is not to say that every activity will have a grade-level associated with it, but it should be fairly easy to tell which ideas would work with older versus younger students.

Number and Operations

By the time a student enters third grade it is hoped, and sometimes assumed, that they will have a good understanding of the meaning behind addition and subtraction, a recall of basic addition facts (with the ability to use these to subtract), as well as some procedure (based on an understanding of tens and ones) to compute with double-digit numbers. We expect this because we know that in third grade students will be computing with three-digit numbers to add and subtract and be introduced to multiplication and division. And, multiplication and division would then be where the majority of time gets spent, in respect to whole number computation. In respect to fractions and decimals, most teachers believe that students will have been introduced to the region model for fractions, as well as the subset of a set model. And, we think that students will understand ideas of halves, fourths, and other commonly used fractions. Again, the reason for this is that these foundational skills will be called upon as more challenging skills are introduced.

Do your students enter your classroom with these skills? Sometimes they do and sometimes they come in with varied levels of understanding and misunderstanding. And, sadly, sometimes these same levels of misunderstanding travel with them into fourth and even fifth grade. We find teachers wondering (often at each grade level) "What did they teach these students last year?" We've both thought it and probably even said it out loud. But the more classrooms we went into the more we began realizing that it's not what "they" taught or didn't teach, but rather how students were taught and whether what was taught had any meaning to students.

Worksheets are not remembered by students and neither are pages of practice problems. But some engaging activity, some interesting problem, and definitely some games will be remembered. And it is more likely that the skills or concepts learned will be remembered and applied later.

The fourth graders in my classroom looked no different from the ones I had taught the year before, or the year before that. But my way of thinking about how to teach these new students had changed. What had changed was that I finally realized that in order to get a clearer idea of how they thought about mathematics and what they knew about mathematics I'd have to "grab" them from the first day of school with an activity that they'd remember for a long time. This was my first day of school activity.

"I wonder," I said to my class as they sat on the floor waiting for the scheduled mathematics lesson to begin, "how many footsteps it would take to walk to Washington, DC." No one said a word. No one raised his or her hand. These students just looked at me—without any real expression. "I'm serious," I said. "If we were going to walk from here to Washington, I wonder how many footsteps we'd take?"

"Don't you ever walk somewhere," I continued, "and you find yourself counting your footsteps? I do it all of the time. Sometimes, I don't even realize that I'm doing it and I smile as I get to 100."

"Yeah, I do that sometimes," Raymond said. And I breathed a silent sigh of relief that someone had responded. "I even count steps when I climb up a big staircase," he continued.

"Thank you for sharing that, Raymond," I replied. "I find myself counting a lot of things and footsteps was what I was hoping you'd help me figure out today. Will you turn to the person who's sitting next to you and talk with them about what you'd need to know in order to figure out how many footsteps it would take to get from here to DC?"

My students seemed a bit confused, a bit quiet, and even a bit uncomfortable with this task. It was, after all, the very first day of school and the rumors flying around the school were that if you got me as your teacher you'd be doing math all day long, and doing some pretty strange things. I guess this was what they expected, but they really didn't know what to expect. They did talk to each other, and the minute or so that I gave to them was just enough for me to make a mental note about who seemed more interested in this question than others.

"If you can hear my voice clap twice," I said (without giving them any indication that I'd be calling their attention by doing something like that). Some stopped talking and clapped two times. And, when others heard them, and I repeated my direction, every student clapped twice. I told them that sometimes I'd get them back from talking with their partner by saying what I'd just said, but sometimes I'd say other things. I told them that they'd have to listen carefully when it was time to come back together as a group.

CLASSROOM-TESTED TIP

When you use Think-Pair-Share, or some other cooperative learning strategy that has students talking together, you need to have a mechanism for getting the students' attention. Silent ways of doing this never worked for us. We'd turn off the lights and children would stop talking, only to begin again as soon as the lights were turned back on. Holding our hands in the air got the attention of several students, but often others continued doing what they'd been doing before hands were in the air. But, clapping, tapping, patting, stomping all seemed to work well in getting students to refocus and get ready to listen. And, by saying things like: clap twice or do a double clap, or clap three times, all reinforced mathematics vocabulary and counting in a way that we felt was important to do.

"So," I said, "What sorts of things did you talk about?"

"We need to know how many miles it is from here to Washington," Jeremy said.

"Who knows about how far it is from Baltimore to Washington?" I asked. Several hands went up. I knew that some of my students had moms or dads who commuted from Baltimore to Washington, DC. I wondered whether their nine-year-old children knew what distance they traveled each day.

"My dad drives to Washington. That's where his office is. It takes him an hour to get to work every day," Bryan announced.

"OK," I said. "So, if he travels about 60 miles an hour how many miles would that be?" Again, hands went up immediately.

"You can't drive sixty miles in an hour going to Washington," Laurie said. "There's lots of traffic. If you could drive that fast for every mile it would be sixty miles. But you can't drive that fast the whole time."

"It could be about fifty miles then!" Kathy said. "Maybe for a little while he has to go a lot slower and it's really only about fifty miles."

I asked the rest of the group whether they were comfortable thinking that the distance between Baltimore and Washington was about fifty miles. Everyone said it was OK. Myra said, "That's a good number anyway. It's a nice number."

"What do you mean it's a nice number?" I asked (hoping that she meant what I wanted her to mean). "It's halfway to one hundred and it's an easy number to use," she said.

"So, now we have an estimate of the distance between Baltimore and Washington. What else did you talk about when you talked with your partner?"

"We need to know how many footsteps a person would walk if they walked for a mile," Laurie said, again.

"We could walk for a mile and count how many footsteps," I heard several children say.

"How will we know how far a mile is?" I asked. "And, what good will that do if we are trying to figure out how many footsteps we'd be taking if we walked all the way to Washington?" I really had perfected the "I'm a bit confused" tone to my voice. And, these fourth graders (who didn't know me very well, yet) were buying it completely.

"Coach told us, last year, that if we walked around the track four times it's a mile," Rhona volunteered. "We could walk around the track!"

I asked the entire class whether they thought that would be a good idea, and all agreed. Luckily this first day of school was a nice day. I assigned partners and asked them whether there were any materials they thought they might need once we got to the track, reminding them that we only had about an hour for math, and walking fifty miles would surely take more than an hour.

One student said that we would have to have clipboards and paper and pencil to write things down. Another said that we might have to have calculators. I didn't even ask them to justify their answers, at this point, I just told them where they could find these materials and they got what they needed and off we went.

"As we walk up to the track," I said to the entire group, "be thinking about the problem we're trying to figure out and what might be a good strategy for getting the answer. We're going to meet, once we get to the track and talk for about a minute before you and your partner begin." I eavesdropped on conversations as we comfortably walked up to the track, feeling very good about the excitement that I felt from these students.

Once at the track we sat down on the grass and I asked them whether anyone had a plan for figuring out the answer to this problem.

Orlando said, "I'm going to be the walker and Charise is going to be the counter. As I take steps she's going to count them for me. Then I won't get confused." Other children seemed to be muttering that this is what they had decided as well. No one mentioned anything about the number of times they would be walking around the track and I decided that this was something I'd just need to observe.

"Before we do this, does anyone want to make a prediction about how many footsteps they think it would be? Go ahead and talk with your partner for about ten seconds and tell your partner how many footsteps you think it will take to get to DC." I let everyone tell me their guesses. Some students seemed to say whatever "big" number they could think of. One hundred thousand was a popular guess, but some students said numbers like "half of a million." I recorded everyone's prediction on the paper I had brought (with my clipboard) and then told everyone that I'd be waiting by the bleachers while they conducted this experiment. Then I watched. And as I watched I smiled broadly as I watched these nine-year-olds slowly walking and counting, in pairs, around the track.

After one lap around several pairs of students sat down on the grass near the bleachers and begin writing things down and using their calculators. I moved from the bleachers to this area and watched and listened as they took the number that had been arrived at (after one lap) and multiplied it by four and recorded their product. I listened and watched as others continued to walk around the track—slowly counting their footsteps. It was so funny to me that the walkers hadn't wondered why the grass-sitters were already done. But, since we hadn't talked about how many times they needed to walk around the track I guessed that they knew what they were doing and felt they needed to walk that full mile.

"What does this number mean?" I asked a pair of students who had finished using their calculator to arrive at the product of 4×367. Not every pair was on the grass with me. Some were still walking around the track, but it didn't seem to matter.

"It's how many footsteps you'd have to take to walk one mile," I heard.

"What do each of those factors represent?" I asked.

"See we didn't want to walk around the track four times. That's a whole mile. So we walked around once and it took 367 footsteps."

"OK," I said, "But how did you know that your other factor was supposed to be four?"

"Remember, we told you that coach told us last year that it was one mile if we went around the track four times. We had to times our 367 by four to get one mile of footsteps," Jal said. I told them that this made perfect sense to me now, and I asked them whether this was the answer to the question.

This same pair told me that now they would have to multiply 1,468 by 50 to show the fifty miles. Then, they explained, we'd know the number of footsteps to walk to Washington. They did this with their calculator and saw the numeral 73,400 and I asked them how to practice saying that number so they could share it with the rest of the class.

Some of the students who had finished this first problem seemed perfectly content to sit on the field and watch their friends walking around the track. I, however, figured that I could pose another challenge to them and see what they did with it. I gathered the group of students around me and I asked them to share their answers. Most were able to say the number on their clipboard without too much difficulty. I knew that without the comma, on the calculator's display, they only had a series of digits to record. So, it was interesting to see who had correctly placed the comma, making the numeral easier to read.

Once they shared their answers I asked them to think about whether it would take more footsteps or fewer footsteps to run to Washington, DC. "Remember," I told them, "It's still the same distance, but instead of walking you'd be running." They talked together and several thought that it would take more footsteps because you'd be "going faster." Other students said that they thought you'd have fewer footsteps because "when you run you take longer steps." I asked them to think of numbers that were greater than their walking numbers, as well as numbers that were less than their walking numbers. And, we talked about numbers while their friends continued walking around the track.

"Can we try it?" these children wanted to know.

"I guess you can," I said, "but as soon as everyone walking is finished I'd like for us all to meet together."

And, as you might imagine, every pair got up and began running. Of course it was more difficult to keep track of the count. But, they were having fun, making predictions, testing them out, and keeping busy—as they thought about what happens when one's stride is longer and the distance remains the same. And, the walkers finally finished, sat down on the grass, and used calculators to figure out how many footsteps it would take to walk fifty miles, to Washington, DC.

About the Math

I could talk a lot about the amazing discussion that followed. And, I could share with you in detail what the "walkers" were thinking as they continued their trek around the track. Some actually did know that they could have only walked once around. They chose to walk around all four times "to be closer to the real amount." Others were, as you might expect, oblivious to the fact that once around meant $\frac{1}{4}$ of a mile, and that they could have then multiplied by 4. But as we discussed this I saw that everyone did a good job listening as their friends shared what they did to get their answers. So everyone was, at least, experiencing different ways to get the answer, and do the experiment.

Did they get the answer to the question? Absolutely! Answers ranged from about 73,000 to close to 100,000. And what were the mathematics connections being made? So many of them that I probably won't get them all. But let me list the connections that I was hoping would be made:

- connecting mathematics to something real—the distance between the city they lived in (Baltimore) and a city that some of their moms and dads worked in (Washington, DC)

- connecting mathematics to geography (it's a bit of a "stretch") as they approximated the distance between these two cities

- connecting physical activity (movement) into the mathematics lesson

- problem solving, reasoning, communicating, and representing a problem's solution

- connecting the mathematics concepts of

    o estimating the quantity of footsteps it would take through predicting

    o counting the number of footsteps it took

    o making sense out of the relationship between the concept of $\frac{1}{4}$ and four times around

    o adding or multiplying (and understanding the concept of each operation in order to use it appropriately)

    o reading and recording multidigit numerals

    o measuring the distance between a walking step and a running step (and then making sense out of the difference—and the impact running would have on the total number of steps)

And, as we walked back to our classroom I couldn't help but wonder: "I wonder how many footsteps it would take to walk from here to New York City?" And I knew that there might be some child who would come to school on the second day with an answer.

Algebra

An important part of algebraic thinking in third through fifth grade is the development of student understanding of patterns and functions. This includes describing and extending geometric and numeric patterns as well as representing and analyzing patterns with words and graphic displays. Students must also learn to express mathematical relationships using equations, and use models and equations to find answers and draw conclusions. Being able to organize data to reveal patterns and functional relationships allows students to also analyze change in various contexts. In the following problem, students are challenged to represent and analyze a situation by constructing various equations.

Activity: Getting 36 Ounces of Tomato Sauce

Mrs. Parker walked to the front of the room with a shopping bag from a local grocery chain and began unpacking the contents. The students were still. As she reached in, their eyes were fixed on the top of the bag waiting to see what was about to be revealed. Inside, there were four cans of tomato sauce. Mrs. Parker stacked the cans from largest to smallest. The tower of sauce included a 30 oz, a 15 oz, an 8 oz, and a 6 oz can. Each can had a label attached with the price and the number of ounces clearly visible.

For a few moments, Mrs. Parker allowed the students to brainstorm their favorite dishes that were prepared with tomato sauce. Then she asked, "What do you notice about the sauce?"

Brad replied, "The cans get smaller and so does the price." She went on to explain that recipes call for a specific amount of sauce, and the cans do not always come in the exact size needed. Mrs. Parker continued by asking students to determine the total amount of sauce when given different combinations, such as two 30 oz cans, three 15 oz cans, or a 15 oz and a 6 oz can. The students responded quickly with the sums for each combination. This was relatively simple for the students to do.

Mrs. Parker then distributed the problem, So Many Options for Sauce, for students to solve (see the form by the same name in the Mathematics Connections in Everyday Experiences on the CD). In the scenario, a boy named Simon and his mother were in the grocery store. She asked Simon to pick up 36 ounces of tomato sauce. As Simon approached the shelf, he saw only 30 oz, 15 oz, 8 oz, and 6 oz cans. Simon must decide which combination of cans to use in order to get 36 ounces of sauce. Mrs. Parker asked the students to consider the problem and see how many different choices they could offer Simon, and which of the choices would be the best to buy.

The students began working while Mrs. Parker circulated around the room to observe. In the first few minutes that they worked the room was rather quiet. But after a few moments, students started sharing with one another at their tables, and recording their combinations to equal 36 ounces of sauce. As a student would express one combination, the others would concur or check to verify the suggestions. They continued working until every student had several combinations equaling 36 ounces. Tiffany organized her answers on a chart (see Figure 6–1).

Others made a list of equations, which included:

$$30 + 6 = 36$$
$$15 + 15 + 6 = 36$$
$$6 \times 6 = 36$$
$$(8 \times 3) + (6 \times 2) = 36$$

So Many Options for Sauce

Simon and his mother are at the grocery store. Simon's mother asks him to get 36 oz. of tomato sauce to put into the shopping cart. Simon looks at the shelf and sees several different can sizes.

30 oz	15 oz	8 oz	6 oz
$1.19	$0.63	$0.35	$0.29

Show Simon some options in choosing cans to equal 36 oz. Then decide which combination is the best choice for his mother to purchase.

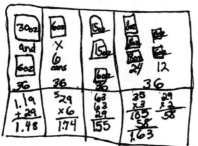

What suggestion would you make to Simon and his mother about the purchase of the sauce? Explain your answer.

My suggestion is 1 can of 30oz and 1 can of 6oz. The total is $1.48. That is cheaper than the other ones.

Figure 6–1 *Tiffany's organized list of answers*

Mrs. Parker got everyone's attention so that a class discussion could begin. She asked several students to display some of the purchasing options on the overhead projector. Children happily came to the front of the room and displayed their collaborative work. Mrs. Parker stood back and watched as her students "took charge" of the lesson. She then asked them how they would decide which combination was the best choice to purchase.

Tiffany shared her finding about price, and concluded that Simon should buy one 30 oz can and one 6 oz can. Emerson agreed with Tiffany and added that it would also be easier to carry just two cans rather than the other combinations of three, five, and six cans. The class also noticed that the more cans used to total 36 ounces, the greater the price, even though it was still exactly 36 ounces. The class concluded that buying the larger cans of sauce was the cheaper choice. To further support this assumption, Melissa found that buying two 15 oz cans and an 8 oz can was still cheaper ($1.61) than six 6 oz cans ($1.74) and you would be getting two extra ounces of sauce. Mrs. Parker asked the class if they thought this was the case with other items in the grocery store as well. She challenged the class to investigate this theory the next time they went food shopping.

About the Math

In this task, students had the opportunity to explore equations equal to a specific value. In the process, students created several equations but considered only those equal to 36 since this would solve the problem. When an equation did not equal 36, the students adjusted their equations accordingly often using the mental computation that they had demonstrated strength in using, earlier in the lesson. In order to choose the best purchasing choice for Simon and his mother, students then had to consider the price of each combination. Students incorporated computational skills of addition and multiplication, both with whole numbers and decimals. They noticed patterns in pricing, and the positive correlation between the increased cost and the number of cans combined to reach the correct total.

Mrs. Parker extended the task even further when she asked students to investigate this trend to see if this was the case with other items in the grocery store as well. Future lessons could highlight the connections with topics such as producers and consumers, as well as discussions of packaging and bulk items. Calculating the unit price for the sauce would also serve as a next step and could be extended to other items such as cereal, juice, paper towels, or shampoo. The real-world connections were authentic and enabled students to recognize the utility of mathematics.

Geometry

There are so many different geometric concepts that students are supposed to make sense out of by the time they are in third grade. Not only are they expected to recognize and name many of the plane figures but they are also supposed to be able to identify attributes of these shapes. This is also true for solid figures, which students have in earlier grades experimented with to determine whether they can roll, slide, spin, or stack. By third grade students are expected to explain what it means for a figure to be congruent, as well as symmetric; they have been introduced to ideas of coordinate geometry. And as students progress through the intermediate grades, these concepts and skills are called upon as they learn to identify acute, obtuse, and right angles, decompose figures as they name parallel and perpendicular line segments, and move into all four quadrants when they do coordinate geometry.

Many teachers admit that if something has to be eliminated from their mathematics program they often don't "do as much geometry" as they should—because there "just isn't enough time." Again this time issue comes up as teachers think about the amount of computational content that they need to teach before their students are assessed.

The elementary experiences that students have in geometry, however, are essential in providing them with the foundational skills needed to make sense out of more formal geometry. And, without these experiences students are, once again, merely trying to remember rules and apply formulas to meaningless problem situations.

By connecting mathematics concepts within one geometry activity a teacher can introduce and reinforce a variety of skills while still allowing students time to explore and manipulate materials. Let's look at an activity done by Ms. Wilson's fourth-grade students. Once we've "seen" what students are doing, we'll not only look at the mathematics in the activity, but look at ways that this same activity can be done with third- and fifth-grade students.

Activity: Creating Plane Figures by Folding a Square

Ms. Wilson began the year with a unit in geometry. She thought that it would give her insight into a different aspect of her students' mathematical thinking—their spatial problem-solving abilities. Hoping to learn what her students already knew she introduced the lesson by holding up an eight-inch by eight-inch square and asking students to think of things that they knew about what she was holding up.

"It's a blue square," Marcus said. "And, it's even a square if you turn it sideways." This was an interesting comment since Ms. Wilson knew (from her colleagues) that students often renamed the square as a "diamond" in the primary grades. She smiled as she told him that this was true, that the square was a square regardless of its position.

"All of the sides are exactly the same," Pria said.

"What do you mean that they are exactly the same?" Ms. Wilson questioned.

"If you measured the sides they would all be the same," Pria said, again. "If the top side of the square was five inches long, then all of the other sides would be five inches long, too."

"Thank you for explaining that to me," Ms. Wilson said. "What else do you notice about this square?"

"It has four right angles," Benjamin offered.

"What is the measure of a right angle?" Ms. Wilson asked him.

"All right angles have ninety degrees," he said proudly. "We learned about this last year."

"Well, you have remembered a lot of important things," Ms. Wilson said, in a complimentary way.

"There are four corners on the square," Randy said.

"Thank you, Randy. Do you know what mathematicians call these corners?"

"I don't remember," Randy answered.

"Why don't all of you turn to a partner and see if you can remember the special term for the corners of a figure," Ms. Wilson told the students.

She listened in on their excited conversations hoping that someone remembered the word *vertex* or *vertices*, but no one did. When she brought the class back together she knew that no one knew.

"This is a word that we are definitely going to add to our 'Mathematics Word Wall,'" she said. "The mathematical name for one of these corners is *vertex* and when there is more than one vertex we call these *vertices*," Ms. Wilson told them. "Does anyone else have something different that you want to say about this square that I'm holding?"

"You could cut it or fold it and make other shapes out of it. We used plastic tangrams last year and all of those pieces make a square," Rachel said.

"Actually, Rachel, you have done a beautiful job of leading right into today's lesson," Ms. Wilson said. "I need everyone to return to your seats. You'll find a large, blue square at your place. We're going to fold this in a special way and see what other shapes we can make." (See the Folding Square Template in the Additional Tools section on the CD.)

Ms. Wilson asked her students to pick up their square and fold it in half so that they had two rectangles. When she saw that each had done this successfully she let them know that they would now be making four more folds. She told them to take one of their vertices and fold it into the center of the square so that it reached the fold that they had just made. (See Figure 6–2.)

Then she asked them to do the same thing with each of the other vertices.

"If you look at the different folds on your square, what are some of the shapes that you can see inside?" Ms. Wilson asked the class.

"There are four triangles," Hassan said. "And they are all the same."

"I see a square inside the triangles," Robert said. "But you have to look around the middle line."

"Here's what I want you to do right now," Ms. Wilson told them. "Take your pencil and trace over the fold lines so you can see more clearly where these lines are. Only do this on one side of your square, so that you don't get confused later on."

Her students carefully traced over the fold lines, either freehand or by using a ruler. This took a bit longer than Ms. Wilson thought it would, but she realized that on the first day of school students were trying to make a good impression. Once they had finished this task she handed each one a recording sheet. (See Folding Square Problem in the Additional Tools section on the CD.)

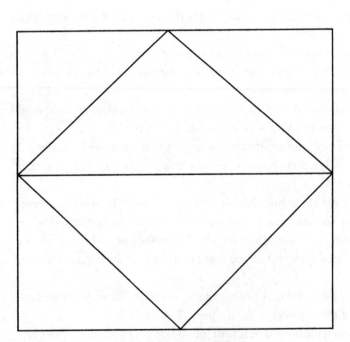

Figure 6–2 *The final product of the folds*

"Here is the problem that I want you to solve today: What are all of the plane figures that you can make by folding along the folds of your square?" (See Figure 6–3.)

As students worked on this problem, Ms. Wilson walked around the room with her clipboard. She wanted to make notes about the strategies that students used. She was looking to see whether children arbitrarily folded, drew, and recorded, or whether they had some systematic way for getting their answers. She noticed that children didn't record the opened square, so she let them know that this was to be counted as one of their figures. After about twenty minutes some students raised their hands to find out whether they had found all of the possible shapes.

"How many did you find?" Ms. Wilson asked.

FOLDING SQUARE PROBLEM

What are all of the plane figures you can make by folding along the folds of your square?

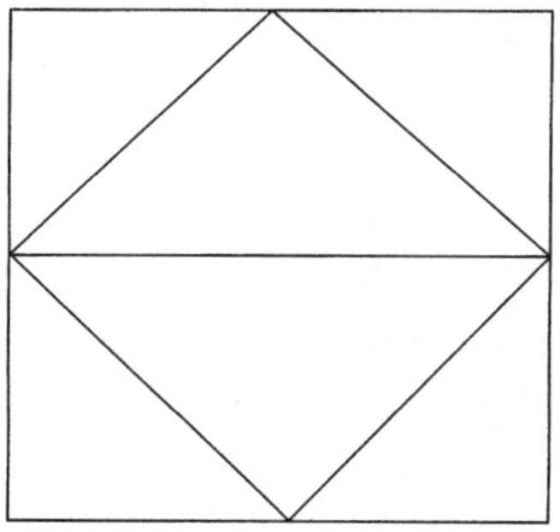

List the figures below.

1._____   6._____

2._____   7._____

3._____   8._____

4._____   9._____

5._____

Figure 6–3 *The problem for students to consider*

"I got five different ones," Jason said pointing to the drawings that he had made on his recording sheet.

"There are more figures that can be made by folding your square along the lines," Ms. Wilson told him, and the others at the table.

This was when students began talking and working together. They began comparing their recording sheets to see if someone had made a different shape than they had made so that they could fold their square and add the figure to their chart. (See Folding Square Answer Sheet in the Additional Tools section on the CD.)

After about thirty minutes Ms. Wilson called the students together and asked them to bring their recording sheets and their squares to the rug. She wanted them to be closer to one another and to her as they discussed the strategies used to solve this problem, as well as the answers to this problem. As each shape was shared every student folded their original square to reproduce this shape. This gave Ms. Wilson a clear view of who was able to do this fairly easily and who seemed to struggle. By the time the discussion was over the lesson had gone on for close to fifty minutes. Ms. Wilson asked her students to put their squares down on the rug and talk with the person closest to them about their findings.

"I noticed that you could make six different shapes with this square," Hassan said.

"What are those shapes?" Ms. Wilson asked the class. Most of the children had their hands raised, since all had just folded these shapes.

"You can make a big and small square. That's one shape," Marcus said. "Then you can make three different pentagons. But that's still just one shape. Then you can make a hexagon, triangle, trapezoid, and a rectangle that isn't a square."

"Does everyone understand what Marcus just said?" Ms. Wilson asked the group.

"He said that we could fold the original square into a rectangle that isn't a square. What does this mean?"

"Last year we found out that a square was a special kind of rectangle," Claudia said. "So, Marcus was talking about the rectangle that we folded that wasn't a square."

Children continued talking about what they had noticed mentioning that if the vertices was four, so were the sides and the number of angles. They wanted to get another recording sheet so they could record their drawings and their information in order from the shape with the fewest sides to the one with the most sides, and Ms. Wilson told them that they could do this for homework that night.

About the Math

Lots of different mathematics concepts and skills were imbedded in Ms. Wilson's first day of school lesson. And, she was also able to diagnose and evaluate many students' spatial problem-solving skills, as well as their persistence and confidence in working on a problem like this.

She learned whether her students were able to:

- recognize and name the six different polygons that they folded

- identify the vertices, sides, and angles of each figure

- use appropriate mathematics vocabulary as they folded their lines and created new shapes

- discuss the attributes of each of the figures

- see beyond or ignore the lines that were drawn and only view the whole figure

- rotate a figure to view it from a different perspective

On the following day, Ms. Wilson used this same square and had her students determine the perimeter of each figure using an inch ruler.

What are other mathematics concepts and skills that could be introduced or revisited with this activity? We felt that fifth-grade students would definitely be able to identify acute, obtuse, and right angles by doing the different folds and identifying the different polygons. The chart that a fifth grader might use could include a column for students to list the different types of angles, as well as a column for the number of parallel sides and perpendicular sides. And, during the review of area and perimeter, this activity could be extended to include determining the area of each figure by using the information about the original square.

Could third-grade students do the folding involved in this activity? Absolutely! This might be something that's done with them later, rather than earlier, in the year. It certainly is something that all students would be capable of doing. We figure that if students are able to fold paper to make "fortune tellers" they would definitely be able to fold a square and use it to make other shapes.

Measurement

Students in third through fifth grade are expected to identify the measurable attributes of objects and the appropriate units associated with each system of measurement. Additionally, they must apply the methods, tools, and procedures required to determine measurements. More specifically, this includes attributes of length, area, volume, weight, and angle size. Within these attributes they further explore notions of standard units (customary and metric) and conversions. Also, students must be able estimate and develop strategies and formulas to determine specific measures. All of these concepts must be explored in an interactive environment.

Students need to be engaged in the process of measurement in order to gain insight into the attributes of an object. The interaction needs to be hands-on. This is best illustrated by James in the following example, which took place in Mrs. Ross' fifth-grade class.

Mrs. Ross began by holding up a cereal box and asking students how they might find the volume of the figure. James immediately called out "length times width times height!" Mrs. Ross was impressed with James' prior knowledge and she handed him the cereal box and a ruler and asked him to explain further.

James positioned the box on his desk and measured the height and length of the front face while Mrs. Ross recorded the dimension on the board. Then James hesitated. He turned the box several times and looks confused. Mrs. Ross asked him what he was thinking, and he responded, "I don't know what else to measure."

After the lesson, Mrs. Ross talked with James and learned that his experiences finding volume were limited to models drawn on paper, with the dimensions already labeled. While James appeared "advanced" when he quickly recalled a formula, he really did not understand the concept of volume, nor had he explored three-dimensional figures in the process.

Exploring the measurement (volume) of three-dimensional figures on a two-dimensional piece of paper seldom builds understanding. This is because instruction of measurement must be interactive. Students really do need to manipulate objects in order to explore their attributes. Mimicking formulas and then practicing them doesn't seem to give students a clear sense of what is really being measured. When they use actual items connections can be made and learning takes place. In the following lesson, students were invited to explore capacity using measuring tools and water.

Activity: Exploring Capacity

Ms. Larson was teaching measurement, specifically capacity, to her fourth-grade students. She wanted them to measure capacity in metric units. The class had already spent some time learning conversions within customary units and she was excited for them to understand that the metric system is based on units of ten, and is much less arbitrary than standard units.

With standard units, students must simply learn that two cups equals a pint, two pints equal a quart, and four quarts equals a gallon. However, with the metric system, the conversions among the units are multiples of tens.

Ms. Larson began by asking the students to consider if it was reasonable for someone to drink a liter of water in a day. Joey responded that it was reasonable because he knew the size of a two-liter bottle, and could image drinking half of the bottle in a day. Ms. Larson revealed a two-liter bottle to the class and they nodded in agreement with Joey. Next, Ms. Larson asked if it was reasonable for someone to drink a milliliter of water in a day. Lisa immediately responded "No way!" Ms. Larson asked Lisa to explain. She said that milliliter sounded like million, and she could not drink a million liter bottles of water in a day.

"Does anyone else hear a familiar part in the word *milliliter*?" Ms. Larson asked.

Jennifer raised her hand and stated, "*Milliliter* starts like *millimeter*, and millimeters are really small, so maybe milliliters are small too." Jennifer made a connection between the metric units of length and the metric units of capacity. Ms. Larson held an eye dropper up for the class to see and explained that it held a milliliter of water. "I could drink lots of those!" called out Lisa.

Ms. Larson distributed capacity kits to groups of three or four students. The kits contained: a milliliter eye dropper, a 30 mL measuring cup, a 250 mL measuring cup (8 oz), a one-liter pitcher, and a two-liter pitcher. She instructed the students to explore the tools and brainstorm an appropriate use for each. After several minutes, each group shared some uses and Ms. Larson wrote their ideas on the chalkboard. They included:

1 mL eyedropper	30 mL cup	250 mL cup	1 L pitcher	2 L pitcher
eye medicine science experiment	cough syrup	drink of juice recipes	soda wash hands	soda water plants fill a bathtub

Ms. Larson explained to the class that they would be using the measuring tools to find the capacity of several containers, but first they needed to discuss how the metric units related to one another. She displayed the sheet Metric Measures for Capacity (see the Connections Among the Content Standards section of the CD for this form) on the projector and reviewed the list of metric units with the students. She then recorded the numeral 1 in the kiloliter column and demonstrated for students that 1 kiloliter = 10 hectoliter = 100 dekaliters = 1,000 liters = 10,000 deciliters = 100,000 centiliters = 1,000,000 milliliters. The students recorded these conversions in a vertical sequence on their papers.

"Oh, that's where the million comes in," said Lisa. Mark held up the liter container and said he was confused because his group's liter container also had 1,000 milliliters recorded at the top. Ms. Larson returned to the next empty column of the recording sheet and wrote 1 in the row labeled liters. She then continued down the column to reveal that 1 liter = 10 deciliters = 100 centiliters = 1,000 milliliters. The students also recorded this information and further discussed the relationship among the units.

Ms. Larson asked, "What about the dekaliters, hectoliters, and kiloliters for one liter?"

Saul answered, "It must be less than one because the numbers are getting smaller."

Nick added, "Maybe it's $\frac{1}{2}$."

Ms. Larson asked, "Do you notice any patterns with the numbers?"

Nick replied, "Yes, when you go down the column, you just add a zero."

Ms. Larson inquired further, "What operation would you use to get an answer like that?"

Mariah said, "Multiply by 10."

Ms. Larson concluded, "Let's test this to see if that works."

Ms. Larson referred to the sheet on the overhead and the students began with kiloliters. They multiply by 10 each time to confirm the conversion to the next unit on the chart.

"So if moving down the chart is like multiplying by 10, what happens if we want to move up the chart?" Ms. Larson asked the class.

After a few moments, Joshua shared that the pattern seen while moving up the chart was the same as dividing by 10. Then Ms. Larson asked several questions relating this to fractions and decimals and the class concurred and concluded that 1 liter = 0.1 dekaliters = 0.01 hectoliters = 0.001 kiloliters.

The students then had the opportunity to measure the capacity of several containers and complete the conversions for each on the chart. Ms. Larson distributed four containers labeled A, B, C, and D to each group, as well as a large pitcher of water. She instructed the groups to find the capacity of each container and record the information on the chart. Then she let them know that once the capacity was found they were to complete the metric conversions. Ms. Larson's final instruction was that the containers did not have to be done in any particular sequence.

The students excitedly reached for containers. Within their groups, they picked a container and discussed which measuring tool would be the most appropriate. Container A was a gallon jug. One group recognized that the capacity was already printed on the label and quickly recorded 3.78 L. The members of each group worked collaboratively to measure the amount of water each container would hold (see Figure 6–4).

As each container's capacity was completed, the students filled in the conversions using the patterns they discussed earlier in the lesson. Ms. Larson circulated around the room posing questions and checking the conversions as the groups worked. Reyna labeled the side of her paper with the operations for the conversions. Although she made a minor error in the number of dekaliters for container B, her conversions were accurate and she understood how to work within the metric units (see Figure 6–5).

Ms. Larson had additional containers available for groups to use if they finished before the others. This was one lesson in which more work (pouring water) did not seem like a punishment for finishing before the others. The students were developing strategies to make the measuring process more efficient. William's group began to fill the containers only half full and then doubled the number of milliliters when recording their answer. Trevor suggested that his group pour the water from container C, which they already completed, into container B and add to it rather than starting over with the water. The group agreed. Ms. Larson requested that the groups share these strategies with the rest of the class throughout the lesson. If she waited until the lesson was over, the students would not have had an opportunity to try a new strategy

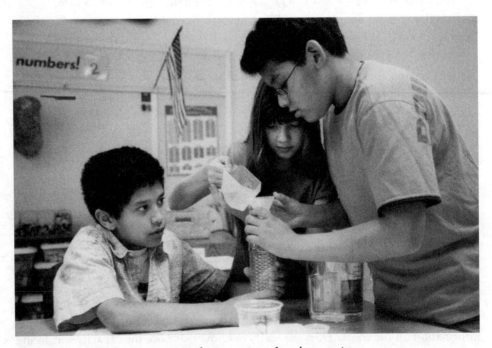

Figure 6–4 *Students measuring the capacity of each container*

Metric Measures for Capacity

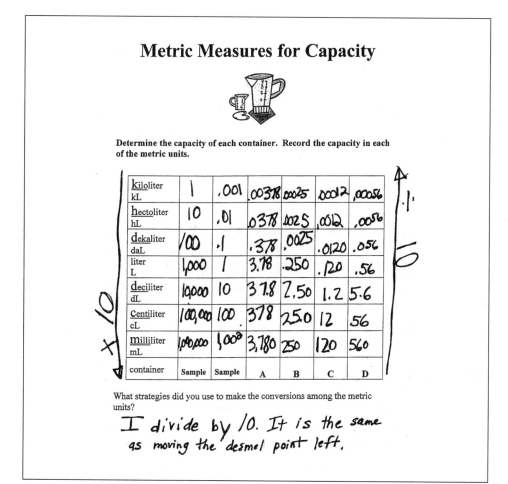

Figure 6-5 *Reyna's record sheet of each container's capacity*

until a later capacity lesson. She wanted to offer them the chance to consider the efficiency of their methods and alter them, if they wanted to.

Once all of the groups had finished finding the capacity of the four containers, Ms. Larson called everyone's attention back to the overhead projector. She asked for volunteers to share the capacity of one of the containers and then the conversions. Kara's group shared that container B held 245 milliliters of water. Ms. Larson recorded the measure on the overhead, and quickly the hands went up and the chatter started.

"That's not what we got," groups exclaimed. Other groups objected as well. Ms. Larson asked each group to announce the number of milliliters they found container B to hold. She recorded the responses on the chalkboard: 245, 250, 252, 250, 244, 245, 250. The dialogue continued.

Ms. Larson asked, "Which is the correct answer?"

Hannah replied, "Two hundred fifty because more groups say so."

Jeremy jumped in with, "But we measured twice, I still think it is 245."

Jerome observed, "Well they're all kinda close."

Ms. Larson posed, "I am certain you all feel like you measured accurately, so what could account for the difference? Take about two minutes and discuss this question within your group."

After two minutes, Ms. Larson called the class back together. Team members shared their thoughts with the class.

Kayla summarized her group's ideas, "Milliliters are real small so we thought it might be easy to be a little off when we measure."

This sparked more discourse and the class ultimately concluded that there could be human error when measurements are taken. Ms Larson added to this by explaining that often the units on measuring tools vary just a little. She said that this could have caused the differences. The students were content with these two explanations and concluded that their answer might be slightly different for each container.

Kara's group completed the conversions for container B and explained that they realized they only had to move the decimal point to the right or to the left depending on whether they were moving up to larger-sized units, or down the chart to smaller units. Carla agreed and said, "The larger the unit, the smaller the number." Groups continued sharing until the chart on the overhead was filled. Ms. Larson collected the materials and told students that she would put a set of materials in a designated spot and during free time students could further practice and explore capacity. They were excited that they might get to do this again.

About the Math

Using the water and containers was so motivating for the students. Having materials to work with enhanced the actual learning of mathematics given the purpose of the lesson. Ms. Larson motivated the students by planning an engaging and interactive experience. She reinforced and instructed many concepts and skills, including:

- reading and writing whole numbers with decimals

- the impact of moving a decimal point on the value of a quantity

- dividing quantities by 10

- multiplying quantities by 10

- measuring capacity in metric units

- converting metric units

- recognizing numeric patterns

The connectedness of these ideas was reinforced through this particular lesson. The students saw the relationship between dividing a quantity by 10 and the affect of the location of the decimal point. The chart format enabled learners to recognize the pattern that existed when converting the metric units due to the operations of division and multiplication. The metric units reinforced the structures of the base ten system. Students made choices about the appropriate tool to use to measure the capacity of each container. Additionally, the class explored the notion that measurements are really just close approximations due to some degree of error in the measuring process and in the tools we use.

Another key element of this lesson, and something for teachers to continually be mindful of, is the development of math vocabulary during instruction. Vocabulary development is particularly important in this lesson because for many students the metric units of capacity are new words. Other than *liters*, Ms. Larson's fourth graders were not familiar with these terms. She added the unit names, as well as *capacity* and *conversions* to her word wall for student reference. Some teachers use mnemonics to help students recall the sequence, according to size, of metric units. These strategies, while often fun for students, must be coupled with a conceptual understanding of conversions and an idea of the relative size of the units. If the latter was missing, students are simply completing a series of operations with no basis for understanding. The conceptual understanding and connections among these ideas provide a strong foundation upon which to build more knowledge.

CLASSROOM-TESTED TIP

Ms. Larson's lesson included a lot of new vocabulary. As young learners, the mathematics we experienced was made up mostly of arithmetic skills. This is no longer the case. A greater presence of geometry, algebra, measurement, statistics, and probability has enhanced the need for vocabulary development in the mathematics classroom. English language learners face additional challenges when confronted with the language of mathematics. Teachers are confronting this issue with a variety of strategies. As in Ms. Larson's case, a word wall serves as an effective instructional practice in building vocabulary skills. She had one word wall in the classroom used for all subject areas. She used color-coded index cards (blue for mathematics) to distinguish between science, social studies, and language arts. The words are arranged alphabetically in columns. The colors help students categorize the words when they are looking for some specific term they need to use.

A different strategy is to record the words on separate charts, by the mathematics concept. Mr. Davis used this approach and had a measurement chart with words such as: *metric, customary, capacity, weight, perimeter, century*. Mr. Davis highlighted the vocabulary words that appeared on several different charts. This reinforced the interconnectedness of mathematics concepts and terminology. All of the charts remained posted throughout the year and were updated as new concepts and skills were explored.

It's important to note that the charts and the word walls are not full when school begins. It isn't until the words are used, in the context of a lesson, that they are added to a chart or to the wall. If they just appeared as a complete chart they might be seen as a decoration in the classroom. But by building it as new ideas are introduced students see the connection to what is being learned.

A third strategy that some teachers use to reinforce vocabulary development is to have students keep personal mathematics dictionaries. Ms. Gibb's fifth-grade students each keep their own mathematics dictionary (housed in the back of their mathematics journal). The last thirty pages are allocated for this and words are arranged alphabetically so that students are able to find them without too much difficulty. Why have thirty pages? We've found that with twenty-six letters in the alphabet we really don't need more than one page per letter. But, the additional four pages are there just in case some letters have more words than can be handled by one page. Ms. Gibb prefers this method because she uses it as an opportunity to reinforce dictionary skills and to learn how to use a reference guide. Vocabulary is recorded along with student-generated definitions. Illustrations are often imbedded in these definitions, along with examples. Here is an entry from Juan's dictionary:

Prime numbers—only factors are one and itself

Example:	Number	Factors
	1	1
	1	1, 2
	2	1, 3
	3	1, 2, 4
	4	1, 5
	5	1, 2, 3, 6

Juan recorded the term and a brief definition and then made a list of integers and tested to see if each was prime. He did this by listing the factors and checking the definition.

Some teachers actually use both personal dictionaries and a word wall in an effort to make the connection between language arts and mathematics, and to help students learn the terminology that is so important in mathematics. Regardless of the format and method, vocabulary development is integral to the development of mathematics understanding and it needs to be reinforced regularly. Knowing this language of mathematics enables students to record, reflect upon, and communicate their understanding.

Data Analysis and Probability

We live in a data-driven society where information is given to us on a regular basis. We are often asked to make decisions and choices based on this information. How is this possible if we don't know how to read, interpret, and analyze the data that we are given? And, in addition to graphs and charts that appear in the media (on the television, in newspapers, and in magazines), we are often given statistics about new medications, products, and even entertainment that may make no sense to us. Advertisers do a pretty terrific job of "selling" us merchandise and employers tell us about median salaries, and we may not know if we are getting a good deal. This is the reality of statistics. But if we help elementary students make sense out of these ideas, through games, activities, and experiments, they connect these school-based understandings to what they hear and see in their world and make better sense of the data that's given to them.

We've done experiments where students take cubes out of a bag (one at a time) and then place them back inside. Based on twenty-five turns they are expected to make a predication about the colors of the ten cubes. This is a good experiment on probability and it can be graphed in a meaningful way. This experiment teaches students many important concepts about interpreting collected data. The activity that we've chosen to share in this last chapter, however, deals with providing students with an experiment that helps them more clearly understand the meaning of *mean, median, mode,* and *range.* Too often these ideas are taught through lists of meaningless numbers and formulas. It's no wonder that students often confuse these levels of central tendency and don't even think about what each term means. Let's look at an activity that was done inside Mr. Lopez's classroom in early February. Knowing that *mean, median,* and *mode* were sure to be on the state assessment, Mr. Lopez felt that the only way to make sure that his fifth graders would remember these ideas would be to conduct an experiment with them. Here's what he did, and here's the impact that this had on his students.

Activity: Links in a Minute

The fifth graders in Mr. Lopez's mathematics class knew that he could come up with "wacky" activities to help them learn new concepts. So, when he poured connecting links onto each table and told his students to explore with them (for several minutes) no one seemed to think that this was at all unusual. He loved watching these "big" kids making "jewelry" out of the links, repeating color patterns and chains. After their exploration time was up he asked them what sorts of things they noticed about this manipulative.

"You can connect the links pretty easily," Sophia offered. "I made a long chain with mine."

"I made an ABCD pattern with mine," Raphael said. "I've got red, blue, yellow, and green over and over again."

"These are really fun to use," Manny said. "We used these a lot in second grade."

"Here's what I need you to do with your links," Mr. Lopez told them. "I need you to disconnect all of your links and put a large pile of them right in front of you." Mr. Lopez watched as his students did this, thinking that it was too bad that the last time they had used them was in second grade. He, himself, could think of so many ways to use this manipulative in mathematics. He gave each student a yellow and a blue sticky note and told them that they also needed to have something to write with. Students took out pencils and listened attentively to his next direction.

"I'm wondering," he said, "how many links you might be able to connect in one minute's time? What I'd like you to do is think about what you just did with the links and write down the number that you think you could connect in a minute. Use your yellow sticky note to record this number."

Students were not allowed to test this out, but only to remember how they connected and disconnected the links that they had explored with. Numerals were recorded on the yellow sticky notes and students were then asked to come to the front of the room, where a horizontal line had been drawn on the white board.

"Who thinks that they have written the largest number on their sticky note?" Mr. Lopez asked his class.

"I wrote 60," Patti said. "I thought that I could do a link a second."

"Did anyone think that they could connect more than one per second?" Mr. Lopez asked the group.

"I thought that I could do about 75," Roger said. "That's more than one each second."

"Did anyone think that they could do more than 75?" No one raised his or her hand. "OK, who thinks that they wrote the smallest number?"

"I only put 30 on my note," Sharon said. "It took me a little bit of time to figure out how to get them together."

"Did anyone have a number that was less than 30?" Mr. Lopez asked. No one raised his or her hand. Mr. Lopez asked his students what the least amount was and the greatest amount. Students answered 30 and 75 and he recorded these numbers on the white board. He put a hyphen between the two and asked the class what the difference between these numbers would be. No one had difficulty saying that it was 45.

He then asked, "Does anyone know the term that mathematicians use for this information?"

"It's called the range," Demetrius answered. "When you figure out the lowest amount and the highest amount and you figure out the difference it's called the range between the numbers."

Mr. Lopez wrote this word on an index card and told the class that he'd add this to their word wall. He then told his students that they'd be making a double line plot that showed their predicted numbers and then their actual numbers, once they had connected their links.

"Let's begin with the lowest number," Mr. Lopez said to his students, "and place this on the end of this line on the left." He asked five students to get up and place their notes on the line where they felt they belonged. Students got up and placed their numbers on the plot. As some got up and realized that their numbers were either less than or greater than others, the numbers got moved around. When all of the numbers had been placed, Mr. Lopez asked whether any of them needed to be moved.

Interestingly enough, these notes were in order, and students had known to place similar numbers in a column.

"What do you notice about this line plot?" Mr. Lopez asked them. Students shared their observations about the number of students who had chosen the number 40 and 50. "It looks to me like people are choosing friendly numbers," he said, reinforcing this expression that had been used when they'd learned strategies to compute without paper and pencil. Children talked about the 75, which they said was an *outlier* and Mr. Lopez asked them to define that term. He then told them that when they returned to their places they would need to place their hands on their shoulders.

"I'll say, '1, 2, 3, go' and you'll be able to begin connecting your links. When I tell you to stop, the minute will be up." Students excitedly returned to their seats and placed their hands on their shoulders, waiting for Mr. Lopez to tell them to begin. When he did they quickly began assembling their links. Except for the clicking of plastic links, the room was silent. The minute seemed long, but when Mr. Lopez said, "Stop!" everyone seemed to moan. He didn't even need to tell them to count their links. Students immediately began doing this and he then asked them to write this amount on their blue sticky note.

"Let's not say how many you were able to connect," Mr. Lopez told them. "Instead, here's what I want you to do. Without talking I want you to stand up and put yourself in order from the shortest to the longest chain."

The students seemed to love this. It was like a game to them. They got up and moved around the room comparing their chains and moving to the left or right of their friends. When everyone seemed to find a place in the line that was made, Mr. Lopez asked each person to say the amount of links that they were able to connect. Students called out their numbers proudly, and when someone found out that they had a lesser amount than the person to their right they moved to their correct spot in the line. Several students said the same number and when the last student said their amount, Mr. Lopez asked whether they could arrange themselves in a different way to see who had the same number of links. All of the students who had the same amounts got in front or in back of each other. From this arrangement, Mr. Lopez could see that three students had been able to put 26 links together and three were able to put 34 links together. There also were two students who each had been able to connect 28, 32, and 35 links.

"Which number of links did the most people connect?" Mr. Lopez asked the class.

"Three people connected 34 links and three people also connected 26 links," Patti said. "Three is the most people."

"Do you know what mathematicians call this information?" Mr. Lopez asked her and the entire group. "When the same amount comes up the most, mathematicians refer to this as the *mode*. And, we have bimodal information, since we have two modes."

"*Mode* and *most* sound almost like the same words," Janetta said. "That's really easy to remember."

"Well, it may be," Mr. Lopez confirmed, "But we are still going to put this word on our word wall." He then had the students return to their straight line and he asked them which quantity of links was right in the middle of their line. Students began saying numbers, but he stopped them to ask if they had some strategy for finding this out. The class came up with different ideas, but it was Raphael who decided that the two end people should both say, "one" together and then the people next to them should say "two" until the person in the middle was left. This happened to work out since Mr. Lopez had twenty-seven students in his class. When the thirteenth students both said, "13" the only person left was the fourteenth student. Mr. Lopez asked this student how many links she was able to connect, and she told him "27."

"So," Mr. Lopez said, "Twenty-seven is the middle number and mathematicians call this the *median*. Now we've found out the median and the mode. I wonder if we could figure out the range?"

Having just done this with their predictions students were able to figure out that the difference between the eighteen that Sara had connected and the thirty-nine that Raphael had connected was twenty-one. Now they knew that the range was twenty-one, the modes were twenty-six and thirty-four, and the median was twenty-seven.

"This is a lot of data that we've collected," Mr. Lopez told the class. "And, I really don't think that it's fair that some people have so many links and some people have so few."

"We could share the links that we got with someone who doesn't have as many," Monica offered. "Then maybe we could all have the same amount."

Mr. Lopez told them that this was exactly what he was going to ask them to do. Students noisily began asking each other for links, and Mr. Lopez seemed to be wondering whether this had been a good idea. It was much more chaotic than he hoped it would be. But after about three minutes of noise, students seemed to settle down and they began to compare their chains again to see if they had the same amount as their friends. The mean had just been found.

Students were directed back to their seats and Mr. Lopez asked them to share the difference between the mean, median, and mode. The discussion went on for about five minutes as these fifth graders wrestled with what each word meant and what had been done to determine each. The final activity involved students coming to the line plot and placing their actual amount onto the plot that had been generated earlier. Because the plot had begun with the predicted number of 30, all of the yellow sticky notes had to be moved so that the first number to the left of the plot could be the eighteen that Sara had connected.

Students sat down on the rug, in the front of the room, for their final discussion of the data on the double line plot. Many different observations were made about the predicted numbers and the actual numbers and the clustering of data around the numbers 25, 27, and 30. They talked about the mean, median, and mode in relation to these numbers and then returned to their desks to write in their mathematics journals some things that they had learned in math that day.

This seventy-five-minute lesson had kept them moving, thinking, talking, and problem solving. No one had appeared bored or disinterested, and Mr. Lopez had noticed that despite the differences in ability levels of his students, all had seemed to understand what had been introduced. This, he believed, had been a very successful lesson, and he hoped that his students would remember these concepts when they saw them on the state assessment.

About the Math

Were you keeping track of all of the concepts and skills that were connected during this lesson? We'll just look at the different mathematics concepts, but you can't forget that movement was a big part of the lesson. For some students, it's what kept them engaged. Getting to move around in math was not something that they did as regularly as they needed to. But with this lesson they were up and down and moving quite a bit. Mr. Lopez made certain that he was:

■ introducing important mathematics vocabulary that dealt with statistics and other number concepts (*nice numbers, range, mean, median,* and *mode*)

■ reviewing ordering numbers from least to greatest

- reinforcing the uses and creation of a double line plot

- helping students determine the difference to find the range

- seeing that students came up with a "silent" strategy to compare lengths of chains

- strengthening students' ability to problem solve in order to determine the median and mean

- providing students with a hands-on, motivating activity that they could remember as they studied statistics and levels of central tendency.

This would be a lesson that he referred to fairly regularly whenever these statistics terms were used. It was not unusual to hear him say, "Remember when we did the links in a minute activity?"

Questions for Discussion

1. What sorts of experiences have you provided for your students that enabled you to teach more than one skill at a time?

2. How have you incorporated writing and vocabulary development into mathematics lessons so that students have a clearer understanding of important mathematics terms?

3. How would you be able to provide longer mathematics periods in order to do some of the lengthier lessons explained in this chapter?

Making Connections

Throughout this book we have given you a rationale for and activities to support making connections in mathematics. Let's return to the original and powerful reason for doing this (aside from the fact that it is strongly advocated by the National Council of Teachers of Mathematics [NCTM]). At the beginning of this book we shared with you the lament that we've heard from many teachers: There isn't enough time. There isn't enough time in the day or in the academic year for teachers to introduce and reinforce all of the content that their state or school system was asking them to teach. "How are we supposed to 'cover' all of this content and still teach in a standards-based manner?" has been said, in many variations, by teachers all over the country.

The demands on a teacher's time and the necessity of preparing students for state assessments have many teachers teaching to the test and foregoing many of the engaging, motivating, and sense-making experiences that they'd like students to have. Yet activities that highlight the connections among the content areas of mathematics actually save teachers time as they weave several different content objectives into one lesson. By doing this a teacher is able to introduce and continually reinforce the grade-level concepts and skills for the year. Knowing the mathematics curriculum and having a variety of resources at their disposal, a teacher can create a lesson in probability while reinforcing ideas involving number. And, when an experiment is devised to test out predictions, students will also get practice in displaying their data in some statistical representation. This can happen in nearly every mathematics lesson, as long as preparation for the lesson includes a careful study of the year's curriculum.

Connections within mathematics concepts and skills provide a meaningful experience for students as they use the skills they've learned in previous years, or earlier in the year, and build on these with newly introduced concepts. The powerful "big idea" of equivalence, which is taught throughout the grades, can be incorporated into so many lessons. And, as a teacher, it's important that you see these connections and make students aware of them. Students are able to deepen their level of understanding when these connections are either pointed out to them or they are given opportunities to find them. A simple question that may help them see these connections could be, "How is what we are learning about equivalent fractions similar to what we've learned about multiplication and division?" If students begin thinking about the identity element for multiplication, and can apply it to forming equivalent fractions, they will move beyond the "rule" of "multiplying the numerator and denominator by the same number." Instead they will see that what they are doing is multiplying by a form of one, and in doing so they are changing the numerals, but not the "idea" of the original fraction. Three-fourths is equivalent to $\frac{9}{12}$ because the original fraction has been multiplied by $\frac{3}{3}$ causing $\frac{3}{4}$ to now have nine out of twelve parts identified.

This network of connections gives students the sense that mathematics is a study where ideas connect to other ideas, and these ideas all make sense. And, when students in fourth and fifth grades use base ten blocks to create arrays to represent multidigit multiplication they are demonstrating a model that will be used later as they take a formal algebra class. Middle school teachers would love for their students to come into their mathematics classes understanding this concept. Solving the following expression: $32 \times 26 = (30 \times 20) + (30 \times 6) + (2 \times 20) + (2 \times 6)$ in this manner prepares a student to solve this expression: $ab \times ac = ?$

Finally, mathematics connections to other areas of the curriculum and to a student's real life enables a teacher to revisit content throughout the year. If the art teacher lets students know that the proportional cartoons that they are creating involve the principle of proportional reasoning, he has given students exposure to the mathematics in art. And, if the music teacher reminds students that the scales they are learning or the patterns that they are identifying are based on the mathematics ideas of patterning and fractions, students see that mathematics is even in the music they are making.

In every discipline there are mathematics connections that can and should be made. But each teacher needs to be aware of these connections and to purposefully identify them and expose students to them. Time is saved teaching measurement skills when a teacher has students carefully measure their fabric as they cut squares and triangles to sew a patchwork quilt. And, when data is collected for a science experiment, a teacher can certainly think about the statistics skills that are being reinforced. In this way, time, during mathematics class, may not have to be used to revisit these skills.

And it just makes sense for teachers to point out to students all of the mathematics that they are using each and every day, even when they aren't in school. Keeping a record of all of these things will help students see that skills overlap and are needed to tell time, shop, estimate distance, and move around in their world. Knowing where to go and how to get there does involve the mathematics of spatial orientation. Students should be made aware of this. When all of these things occur, a teacher will never hear his or her students say that the only time they'll be using mathematics over the weekend is when they do their mathematics homework. And, when this is done, students will see mathematics as being essential to their lives, now and in the future.

Questions for Discussion

1. In your school, and your students' grade level, how are connections reinforced in each of the content areas?

2. What is your role in preparing students with the skills that they need to move easily into the next grade level?

3. How does the integration of the process standards, with the content standards, enhance students' learning?

4. Why is vocabulary development so important in the teaching of mathematics?

Additional Resources for Connections

The following resources are meant to support you as you continue to explore the connections standard in grades 3 through 5. You will find a variety of text resources—books that will provide you with additional connections or instructional strategies. A list of math websites is included to supply you with problem tasks, electronic manipulative ideas, or teacher resources.

Text Resources

The following text resources provide a variety of activities and strategies for supporting students as they develop connections:

AIMS Series. Grades K–6. Fresno, CA: AIMS Education Foundation.

Fennell, F., H. Bamberger, T. Rowan, K. Sammons, and A. Suarez. 2000. *Connect to NCTM Standards 2000: Making the Standards Work at Grade 3*. Chicago, IL: Creative Publications.

———. 2000. *Connect to NCTM Standards 2000: Making the Standards Work at Grade 4*. Chicago, IL: Creative Publications.

———. 2000. *Connect to NCTM Standards 2000: Making the Standards Work at Grade 5*. Chicago, IL: Creative Publications.

National Council of Teachers of Mathematics. 1989. *Curriculum and Evaluation Standards for School Mathematics*. Reston, VA: Author.

———. 1991. *Professional Standards for Teaching Mathematics*. Reston, VA: Author.

———. 1995. *Assessment Standards for School Mathematics*. Reston, VA: Author.

———. 2000. *Principles and Standards for School Mathematics*. Reston, VA: Author.

———. 2006. *Curriculum Focal Points for Prekindergarten Through Grade 8 Mathematics*. Reston, VA: Author.

This series of books provides teachers at each grade level (K–8) with ideas for lessons that are standards based. Each book provides explanations of how the standards relate to specific lessons (twenty ready-to-teach lessons)—complete with teaching plans, reproducible pages for student activities, helpful suggestions for assessing students' understanding, and ideas for extending lessons. Each chapter also provides teachers with ideas for taking textbook lessons and making them more standards based.

Nelson, D., G. G. Joseph, and J. Williams. 1993. *Multicultural Mathematics: Teaching Mathematics from a Global Perspective.* Oxford, England: Oxford University Press.

This book is about teaching mathematics from a multicultural or global perspective. The first few chapters provide a rationale for using an approach of this nature, along with a collection of examples demonstrating how such an approach can be applied within and throughout the school curriculum. In the remaining chapters, the authors provide greater details about topics, in elementary arithmetic, geometry, algebra, and statistics that can be incorporated into a mathematics program.

Vogt, S. 1994. *Multicultural Math: Combine Cultural and Historical Awareness with Mathematical Concepts.* Greensboro, NC: Carson-Dellosa Publishing.

This book assists teachers in promoting cultural and historical awareness with mathematical concepts introduced to students in grades 1 through 4. There are activities exploring the history of time, problem-solving activities using other numeration systems, and games from many countries. The reproducibles in the book make it easy for teachers to use with students.

Vogt, S. 1993. *Linking Math & Literature: Critical Thinking Activities for 35 Literature Titles, Grades 4–6.* Cypress, CA: Creative Teaching Press.

Many of the thirty-five books featured in this resource book are award-winning pieces of children's literature. The activities suggested link mathematics with practical everyday experiences—using good children's literature. Most of the activities promote a student's ability to reason and solve problems, as well as think critically. There are some reproducibles and answers at the end of the book.

Thiessen, D., and M. Matthias, eds. 1992. *The Wonderful World of Mathematics: A Critically Annotated List of Children's Books in Mathematics.* Reston, VA: NCTM.

This resource book provides teachers with over 500 listings of children's literature books that could be used as a part of a mathematics lesson. While some may be for primary students, many could be used in third- through fifth-grade classrooms. A brief synopsis of each book is given, as well as its price, the concept(s) it reinforces, and the age of student it is appropriate for.

Braddon, K. L., N. J. Hall, and D. Taylor. 1993. *Math Through Children's Literature: Making the NCTM Standards Come Alive.* Englewood, CO: Teacher Ideas Press.

When it was first released, this wonderful resource book provided teachers with a list of out-of-print pieces of math-related literature, claiming that every selection it would be reviewing was "in print." Unfortunately this book is now dated and some of the selections are now out of print. But it is still an excellent resource for teachers to use. Titles are given, as well as a brief summary of the selection. Activities are provided, as well as some reproducibles to use. The books are separated by content standards with listings of K–3 selections and then 4–6 selections, making it easy to sort out the primary books from those used more effectively with older students.

Websites

Social Studies and Multicultural Connections

www.sofweb.vic.edu.au/litnumweek/eys/games/traditional/hopscotch.htm
www.sofweb.vic.edu.au/litnumweek/eys/games/traditional/dominoes.htm
www.ga.k12.pa.us/academics/us/math/gcometry/stwk98/JENLR2/rith.htm
www.ga.k12.pa.us/academics/us/math/geometry/stwk98/JENLR2/topedi.htm
http://imagiware.com/mancala
http://score.kings.k12.ca.us/lessons/poneyexp.htm
http://sin.fi.edu/time/keepers/Silverman/html/RomanMatch.html
http://worldatlas.com/webimage/countrys/nariv.htm

Technology and Mathematics

Online Manipulatives

http://nlvm.usu.edu/en/nav/vlibrary.html

Interactive Websites

www.uen.org/3-6interactives/math.shtml
www.bbc.co.uk/schools/numbertime
www.iknowthat.com/com/L3/Area=L2_Math

Resources

www.mathforum.org/te
http://people.clarityconnect.com/webpages/terri/terri.html
http://mathstories.com/
www.mathcounts.org
http://illuminations.nctm.org
http://teacher.scholastic.com/ilp/index.asp/SubjectID=3
http://themathworksheetsite.com
http://visualmathlearning.com
www.internet4classrooms.com/math_elem.htm

Literature and Mathematics

www.education-world.com/a_curr/curr249.shtml
www.education-world.com/a_tech/tech016.shtml

Art and Mathematics

www.enchantedmind.com/puzzles/tangram/tangram.html
http://syrylynrainbowdragon.tripod.com/tes.html
http://log24.com/theory/dd/netsVersion.html
http://euler.slu.edu/teachmaterial/hyperlinks_for_geometry.html
http://mathforum.org/~sarah/shapiro
www.mathartfun.com

Music and Mathematics

www.lessonplanspage.com/MathMusicMultiplicationFacts24.htm
www.songsforteaching.com
www.songsforteaching.com/mathsongsadvanced.htm
http://library.thinkquest.org/4116/Music/music.htm

Science and Mathematics

www.aimsedu.org/index.html
http://oregonstate.edu/pubs/ssm
www.canton.edu/employee/gfellerm/NaturalConnection.pdf
www.fi.edu/htlc/teachers/wilkes/planafter.htm
www.k12academics.com/why_integrate_math.htm

Bellon, J., E. Bellon, and M. Blank. 1992. *Teaching from a Research Knowledge Base*. New York: Merrill (imprint of Macmillan), 277–79.

Berlin, D. F. 1991. *Integrating Science and Mathematics in Teaching and Learning: A Bibliography*. School Science and Mathematics Association Topics for Teachers Series, No. 6. Columbus, OH: ERIC Clearinghouse for Science, Mathematics, and Environmental Education.

Berlin, D. F., and A. L. White. 1995. Connecting School Science and Mathematics. In P. A. House and A. F. Coxford, eds., *Connecting Mathematics Across the Curriculum*, 22–33 Reston, VA: NCTM.

Braman, A. N. 2000. *Traditional Native American Arts and Activities*. New York: John Wiley and Sons.

Bright, G. W., and J. M. Joyner, eds. 1998. *Classroom Assessment in Mathematics: Views from a National Science Foundation Working Conference*. Lanham, MD: University Press of America.

Burnett, J., and Calvin Irons. 1996. *Nature's Mathematical Marvels*. San Francisco, CA: Mimosa Publications.

———. 1997. *Mathematics on the Move*. San Francisco, CA: Mimosa Publications.

Burns, M. 1992. *Math and Literature* (K–3). Sausalito, CA: Math Solutions Publications.

———. 1994. *The Greedy Triangle*. New York: Scholastic, Inc.

Countryman, J. 1992. *Writing to Learn Mathematics*. Portsmouth, NH: Heinemann.

D'Ambrosio, U. 1985. "Ethnomathematics and Its Place in the History and Pedagogy of Mathematics." *For the Learning of Mathematics* 5: 44–48.

Davies, A. 2000. *Making Classroom Assessment Work*. Courtenay, British Columbia: Classroom Connections International Inc., 13.

Donaldson, M. 1979. *Children's Minds*. New York: Norton.

Fosnot, C. T., and Maarten Dolk. 2001. *Young Mathematicians at Work: Constructing Number Sense, Addition, and Subtraction*. Portsmouth, NH: Heinemann.

Griffiths, R., and M. Clyne. 1991. *Books You Can Count On*. Portsmouth, NH: Heinemann.

Higgins, J. L. 1988. "One Point of View: We Get What We Ask For." *Arithmetic Teacher* 35 (5): 2.

House, P. A., and A. F. Coxford, eds. 1995. *Connecting Mathematics Across the Curriculum*. Reston, VA: NCTM.

Irons, C., Tom Rowan, Honi Bamberger, Anna Suarez. 1998. *Meaningful Mathematics Module 1*. San Francisco, CA: INSIGHT (a division of Mimosa Publications).

McCoy, L., and J. Shaw. 2003. "Patchwork Quilts: Connections with Geometry, Technology, and Culture." *Mathematics Teaching in the Middle School* 9 (2): 46–50.

Murphy, S. 2004. *Divide and Ride.* New York: Scholastic.

Nahrgang, C. L., and B. T. Peterson. 1986. "Using Writing to Learn Mathematics." *The Mathematics Teacher* 79 (6): 461.

National Action Council for Minorities in Engineering, Inc, National Council of Teachers of Mathematics, Widmeyer Communications. 2001. *FigureThis! Math Challenges for Families.* Reston, VA: NACME.

National Council of Teachers of Mathematics. 1991. *Professional Standards for Teaching Mathematics.* Reston, VA: Author.

———. 1993. *Assessment in the Mathematics Classroom.* (Norman L. Webb and Arthur F. Coxford, Eds., Reston, VA: NCTM.

———. 1995. *Assessment Standards for School Mathematics.* Reston, VA: Author.

———. 2000. *Principles and Standards for School Mathematics.* Reston, VA: NCTM.

Nichols E. D., and Sharon L. Schwartz. 1999. *Mathematics Dictionary and Handbook.* Honesdale, PA: Nichols Schwartz Publishing.

Oberdorf, C. D., and Jennifer Taylor-Cox. 1999. "Shape Up!". *Teaching Children Mathematics* 5(6): 340–45.

Onyefula, I. 2000. *A Triangle for Adaora: An African Book of Shapes.* New York: Dutton Children's Books.

Stenmark, J. 1989. *Assessment Alternatives in Mathematics: An Overview of Assessment Techniques That Promote Learning.* Berkeley, CA: EQUALS, Lawrence Hall of Science.

Thomson, M., and D. William. 2005. "Classroom Assessment Minute by Minute, Day by Day." *Educational Leadership* 63 (3): 19–24.

Wachowiak, X., and R. D. Clements. 2006. *Emphasis Art: A Qualitative Art Program for Elementary and Middle Schools,* (8th ed.) Boston, MA: Allyn & Bacon.

Welchman-Tischler, R. 1992. *How to Use Children's Literature to Teach Mathematics.* Reston, VA: NCTM.

Wyatt, V. 2000. *The Math Book for Girls and Other Beings Who Count.* Tonawanda, NY: Kids Can Press, Ltd.

Zaslavsky, C. 1979. *Africa Counts: Number and Pattern in Africa Culture.* Brooklyn, NY: Lawrence Hill Books.

Why Are Activities on a CD?

At first glance, the CD included with this book appears to be a collection of teaching tools and student activities, much like the activities that appear in many teacher resource books. But rather than taking a book to the copier to copy an activity, the CD allows you to simply print off the desired page on your home or work computer. No more standing in line at the copier or struggling to carefully position the book on the copier so you can make a clean copy. And with our busy schedules, we appreciate having activities that are classroom ready, and aligned with our math standards.

This CD gives you much more than a mere set of activities. It gives you the power to create an unlimited array of problems that are suited to your students' interests, needs, and skills. Have fun! Get creative! And design problems that stimulate your students' curiosity and push their skill development. Following are a few examples that provide you with some ideas of ways to make the most of the editable feature on the CD. Whether your goal is to engage and motivate your students or to differentiate the activities to meet your students' needs, the CD will allow you to easily adapt each problem. Simply rename the file when saving to preserve the integrity of the original activity. A more complete version of this guide with more samples for editing the activities can be found on the CD-ROM.

Editing the CD to Motivate and Engage Students

Personalizing Tasks or Capitalizing on Students' Interests

The editable CD provides a quick and easy way to personalize math problems. Substituting students' names, the teacher's name, a favorite restaurant, sports team, or location can immediately engage students. You know the interests of your students. Mentioning their interests in your problems is a great way to increase their enthusiasm for the activities. Think about their favorite activities and simply substitute their interests for those that might appear in the problems.

In the second version of the example that follows, the teacher knows that many of her students play basketball at recess and decided to reword the task to capture their interest. Using the editable forms to make these simple changes to the problem task allows her to create a version of the problem that works best for the students. *Note:* This type of editing is also important when the problem situation may not be culturally appropriate for your students (i.e., students in your class may not typically attend family reunions).

Name _____

More Spaghetti and Meatballs

After reading *Spaghetti and Meatballs for All* by Marilyn Burns, Mrs. Hittle's class decided to plan their own family reunion. If each of the 7 square tables seats 4 people (one on each side of the table), then how can the tables be arranged to seat *exactly* 24 guests?

Show your work

Explain how you solved the problem.

_____
_____
_____
_____
_____
_____

Challenge: If every seat was filled for the dinner and the cook made $\frac{1}{4}$ lb. of pasta for each person, how many pounds of pasta did he cook?

Show your work.

Name _____

The Basketball Benefit

The Maryvale Movers basketball team is planning a spaghetti dinner to raise money for new uniforms. The team is arranging the tables for the event. If each of the 7 square tables seats 4 people (one on each side of the table), then how can the tables be arranged to seat *exactly* 24 guests?

Show your work.

Explain how you solved the problem.

_____
_____
_____
_____
_____

Challenge: If every seat was filled for the dinner and the cook made $\frac{1}{4}$ lb. of pasta for each person, how many pounds of pasta did he cook?

Show your work.

Editing the CD to Differentiate Instruction

Creating Shortened or Tiered Tasks

While many students are able to move from one task to another, some students benefit from focusing on one task at a time. By simply separating parts of a task, either by cutting the page into two parts or by using the editable CD feature to put the two parts of the task on separate pages, teachers can help focus students on the first part of the task before moving them to part two. Teachers might choose to provide all students with the first task and then give students the second part after they have completed, and had their work checked by the teacher. In this sample, in which the two parts of the task initially appeared on one page together, the tasks have been separated and the lines for writing responses are wide for students who may need more writing space.

Name _____

Packing for Camp

Kevin was packing for a camping trip. His suitcase included the following:

- green shorts
- jean shorts
- tan pants
- black pants
- striped shirt
- plaid shirt
- red shirt
- blue shirt
- white shirt

1. How many different possible outfits could Kevin choose from his suitcase (each outfit must include either pants or shorts, and a shirt)?

Show your work.

Name _____

Packing for Camp

Kevin was packing for a camping trip. His suitcase included the following:

- green shorts
- jean shorts
- tan pants
- black pants
- striped shirt
- plaid shirt
- red shirt
- blue shirt
- white shirt

2. If Kevin reaches into his suitcase and randomly pulls out an outfit, what is the probability that his outfit will include a pair of shorts and either a striped or a plaid shirt? Record your answer as a fraction, a decimal, and a percentage. Show your work.

Fraction: _____ Decimal: _____ Percent: _____

Modifying readability of tasks

Adding some fun details can generate interest and excitement in story problems, but you might prefer to modify some problems for students with limited reading ability. While the problems in version #2 below are the same as in the previous version, the tasks are written in simpler ways to support those students who might benefit from fewer words and simpler vocabulary. Simply deleting some of the words on the editable CD will result in an easy-to-read version of the same task.

Name _____

Food Shopping

Mrs. Barnes went to the grocery store to do some food shopping for her family. She never realized there was so much mathematics involved in this activity. Help Mrs. Barnes complete her food shopping.

Produce Section

1. Mrs. Barnes purchased 3 pounds of grapes. The grapes sold for $2.99 per pound. How much did she spend on the grapes?

   _____

   Show your work.

Bakery Department

2. Mrs. Barnes volunteered to provide rolls for the neighborhood picnic. She needs enough rolls for 45 people. If there are 8 rolls per package, how many packages of rolls must she buy?

   _____

   Show your work.

Check-Out

3. The total cost of her food order was $23.79. If Mrs. Barnes paid with 2 twenty dollar bills, how much change will she receive?

   _____

   Show your work.

Name _____

Food Shopping

1. Mrs. Barnes purchased 3 pounds of grapes. The grapes sold for $2.99 per pound. How much did she spend on the grapes?

   _____

   Show your work.

2. She needs enough rolls for 45 people. If there are 8 rolls per package, how many packages of rolls must she buy?

   _____

   Show your work.

3. The total cost of her food order was $23.79. If Mrs. Barnes paid with 2 twenty dollar bills, how much change will she receive?

   _____

   Show your work.

Modifying Data

While all students may work on the same problem task, modifying the problem data will allow teachers to create varying versions of the task. Using the editable CD, you can either simplify the data or insert more challenging data including larger numbers, fractions, decimals, or percents.

Name _____

Family Measures of Central Tendency

Northwood Elementary School plans many family events throughout the year, and gathered more information about the size of the families in order to better prepare when buying and gathering materials for family nights.

The following data was collected from several families regarding the number of family members in one household:

3, 5, 4, 2, 4, 4, 6, 4, 5, 4, 3, 5, 5, 4, 7

Find the mean. Show your work.

Find the median. Show your work.

Find the mode. Show your work.

1. How would you describe the size of the families revealed in the data collected?

_____

_____

2. Survey 10 classmates to find the number of people living in their household. Use the data to find the mean, median, and mode.

_____

_____

_____

Name _____

Family Measures of Central Tendency

Northwood Elementary School plans many family events throughout the year, and gathered more information about the size of the families in order to better prepare when buying and gathering materials for family nights.

The following data was collected from several families regarding the number of family members in one household:

3, 5, 4, 2, 4, 4, 6, 4, 5, 4, 3, 5, 5, 4, 7, 6, 3, 5, 4, 2

Find the mean. Show your work.

Find the median. Show your work.

Find the mode. Show your work.

1. How would you describe the size of the families revealed in the data collected?

_____

_____

2. Survey 25 classmates to find the number of people living in their household. Use the data to find the mean, median, and mode.

_____

_____

_____